D1156695

'SHAW DIVINITY SCHOOL LIBRARY

Archaeology
and the Living Word

ARCHAEOLOGY AND THE LIVING WORD

JERRY VARDAMAN

BROADMAN PRESS
Nashville, Tennessee

© 1965 • Broadman Press
All rights reserved

422–258

DEWEY DECIMAL CLASSIFICATION: 220.93
Library of Congress catalog card number: 65–15599
Printed in the United States of America

12.F65KSP

Preface

▲▲▲

Writing a comprehensive, up-to-date account of biblical archaeology is almost impossible. Archaeological discoveries continue to be made in such rapid-fire fashion that new books on this subject are needed as soon as the latest ones are published. Also, the field of biblical archaeology is now so complex and specialized that a definitive work would require the cooperative effort of hundreds of scholars. Hence selectivity is necessary.

Some of the guiding principles in choosing the materials to be discussed include: (1) A proper balance between Old and New Testament archaeological discoveries; (2) the more significant and solidly established results of archaeological research; and (3) the more recent discoveries.

For photographs illustrating the various discoveries, the reader is referred to J. B. Pritchard's *The Ancient East in Pictures Relating to the Old Testament* (Princeton: Princeton University Press, 1954). Many useful pictures which relate to the New Testament may be found in *The Good News: The New Testament with Over 500 Illustrations and Maps* (New York: The American Bible Society, n.d.).

The author gratefully acknowledges appreciation to Mrs. Glenn Hinson for typing the finished copy of this book; Mrs. Rodney Hale for typing the rough draft of the book from the original manuscript; and to the Administrative Services Office of the Southern Baptist Theological Seminary for help at numerous points. William Fallis of the Broadman Press has made valuable suggestions. To the authors and publishers who have granted permission to quote from their material, due appreciation is expressed.

JERRY VARDAMAN

Contents

▲▲▲

Contents

1

The Value of Biblical Archaeology

▲▲▲

Recent years have seen much public interest in the Bible. Sometimes this interest has been created by legal decisions related to the question of Bible reading in the public schools. At other times, it has fixed on whether biblical teachings forbid or can be accommodated to the theory of biological evolution. Also, there have been several new translations of the Bible into English in the last decades. Claims about the merits or failings of these new translations have focused much publicity on the Bible.

Biblical archaeology, also, has been responsible for much of the modern interest in the Bible. Publishers have detected a shift of reading interests toward books which deal with archaeology. Books on biblical archaeology (like Millar Burrows, *The Dead Sea Scrolls* and Werner Keller, *The Bible as History*) frequently become "best sellers." Since the end of World War II, new archaeological discoveries have made it almost impossible even for specialists to stay abreast.

In spite of the frustration involved, this fact should cause great rejoicing among those who love the Bible. Only a hundred years ago, certain phases of biblical study were, in many respects, like "locked doors," which "no man could open." This does not mean that the Bible was veiled in such mystery that its basic message was unclear. But many problems of

Bible history, geography, chronology, and so on simply appeared to have no answer. Archaeology has provided a key to open some of these doors, at least part way.

Archaeology aids in the location of the geographical sites of the Bible.—Slightly over a century ago the geographical references of the Bible were grossly misunderstood. It is easy to understand, for example, why Luther would say in the preface to his translation of the prophecies of Isaiah: "It would be nice also to know how the [biblical] lands were situated with reference to one another, so that the strange unfamiliar words and names might not make reading disagreeable and understanding puzzling and hard."

One of the first scientific students of Palestinian geography was Edward Robinson. With Eli Smith, a missionary stationed at Beirut, Robinson carried out two epoch-making surveys (1838; 1852) of Sinai, Palestine, Galilee, and Lebanon (ancient Phoenicia), which greatly clarified the place names of the Bible. Robinson was thoroughly acquainted with all of the older literature which related to the holy places. He used clues which presented themselves in examining these sites firsthand, such as definite evidence that a site was ancient.

Robinson also made use of the Arabic names by which these places are called. He reasoned that the older biblical names would tend to be preserved in the modern Arabic names. For example, he correctly identified the biblical site of Gibeon, which was called "el-Jib" in his day, as it still is. That he was correct has been confirmed by several inscribed jar-handles, found there in excavations. The letters "GB'N" were written in ancient Hebrew on these handles from broken wine jars. This form of spelling (without vowels) was the same way, of course, that the name Gibeon was spelled in the biblical period. Robinson made numerous other identifications and has rightly been called the "father of Palestinian geography."

A few decades after Robinson, an extensive survey was carried on in western Palestine which resulted in a work titled *Map of Western Palestine in 26 Sheets* (London: P. E. F., 1880). Students now had available for the first time a truly scientific map of the country. Hundreds of new identifications of forgotten biblical sites resulted, for the map had over six thousand places identified. The value of this map has not diminished in the passing years, though revision, naturally, has gone on as new discoveries have come to light.

Geographical references abound in the New Testament, especially in the itineraries of Paul's missionary journeys. The major cities which Paul first visited in Asia Minor are named in Acts 13–14: Attalia, Perga, Antioch in Pisidia, Iconium, Lystra, and Derbe. With rare exceptions (Attalia and Iconium), the location of these places had been entirely forgotten before 1800. The romance of their rediscovery is a thrilling chapter in archaeology.

William M. Leake, the famous student of classical geography, made two trips to Asia Minor (1805, 1820). He wrote that "of the cities, which the journey of St. Paul has made so interesting to us, the site of one only (Iconium) is yet certainly known. Perga, Antioch in Pisidia, Lystra, and Derbe, remain to be discovered." Leake made a suggestion for Perga's location, which later was proved by inscriptions to be accurate.

In 1832, Lord Arundell, a British chaplain stationed at Smyrna, similarly located Antioch of Phrygia (more popularly known as Antioch in Pisidia) by inscriptional evidence. In 1884–85, a scholar who later became professor of Greek at Cornell University, J. R. S. Sterrett, established the position of Lystra. Again, the problem was settled by an inscription. Such archaeological evidence makes possible the accurate location of these long-forgotten biblical places, when all other lines of investigation fail or leave the student uncertain.

Archaeology assists in fixing the chronology of biblical events.—Edwin Thiele has correctly observed that "chronology is the backbone of history." To understand and to interpret correctly the various incidents recorded in the Bible requires that the student first be able to determine the proper sequence of such events. Quite often valuable data is gained through the discovery of archaeological materials, which supply key historical facts.

It will be helpful at this point to illustrate archaeology's part in biblical chronology. All textbooks on biblical history written before 1923 listed 606 B.C. as the date of Nineveh's destruction. In 1923, C. J. Gadd published new documentary evidence which demonstrated positively that Nineveh fell in 612 B.C. The new historical source which established this pivotal date was known as the "Babylonian Chronicle." It gave a full account of the last days of the Assyrian Empire and mentioned the last Assyrian kings. New portions of this document mention the sequence of events which led to Nebuchadnezzar's conquest of Jerusalem in 597 B.C.

Biblical archaeology provides light on culture and customs. —It is amazing to see how well the Bible fits against the cultural background of the ancient Near East. Archaeology has provided the information. The following example shows how dramatically it has changed some views. Wellhausen, a writer who was once quite influential, declared in 1878 that very little worth could be attached to the narratives about the patriarchs. Yet, in recent years, new discoveries tend to demonstrate the opposite. The customs of inheritance, adoption, religious practices, purchase of property, and so on, reflected in the patriarchal narratives, fit perfectly against their Near Eastern background. Thus, we see that older critics frequently were mistaken on various points of interpretation concerning the patriarchs.

The Gospel of John mentions that Jesus was buried according to the "custom" of the Jews (cf. 19:40). Archaeologists have gathered enough information concerning first-century Jewish burial practices to give a step-by-step account of what was done.

The burial place consisted of a chamber hollowed out of a rock hillside. On stone ledges within such tombs, the dead would be stretched out and wrapped in bandage-like strips of linen. Within the folds of these cloth bands, spices were placed. These served to retard the foul odors engendered by the decomposition of the body.

Moreover, in the time of Jesus, Jewish funerals were notoriously expensive. Thus, it was perfectly in order for Nicodemus to bring a mixture of a hundred *litras* of myrrh and aloes (equals about 75 pounds; see John 19:39). After bodies decomposed, the bones which remained would be gathered by the family and placed in little bone-caskets (called "ossuaries"). The size of these bone-caskets (usually around twenty inches long) was determined by the length of the longest bone in the body, the femur. The deceased's name would be scratched on his bone-casket, which was then placed in one of the niches (resembling a miniature tunnel) that led off from the main burial chamber.

Many Jewish ossuaries have been recovered in recent years, and the names they bear correspond with personal names mentioned in the Gospels. In other words, the complete description of Jesus' burial fits his time exactly. Every detail harmonizes with the archaeological evidence.

Archaeology provides new sources of information on the historical background of the Bible.—The Bible has an inescapable relationship to history. It consists of various writings which were produced in widely scattered places—Palestine, Egypt, Babylon, Greece, Rome, Asia Minor—over centuries of time. Each biblical author lived at a definite point in history and was forced to grapple with specific dangers, temptations, or problems. Through archaeological research, new historical sources fill in the gaps and enable the modern world to see more clearly the various issues which challenged the biblical writers.

It is easy to expect too much, of course. Understandably, many of the individual literary expressions of the Bible are veiled in mystery. Recovering the obscure circumstances which prompted individual laments or expressions of praise in certain psalms, for example, remains unlikely. But the broad sweep of biblical history is now well understood. Continuing discoveries add new dimensions to vague references which once seemed impossible to understand.

Sargon was a definite historical character. Yet for centuries the only historical source of information available on this Assyrian king was the reference to him in Isaiah 20:1. In 1843, the French archaeologist, Paul-Emile Botta, excavated the elaborate palace which Sargon had constructed at his new capital of Dur-Sharrukin—the Citadel of Sargon, built in 706 B.C. Detailed written records show that the walls of this royal palace, located about twenty miles north of Nineveh, were decorated with numerous artistic reliefs.

Sargon's monuments describe the bloodshed, courage, and triumphs (never defeats!) of his mighty armies. His record of the capture of Samaria (721 B.C.) adds color and new information to the parallel biblical account (cf. 2 Kings 17:5–41).

Sargon's capture of Ashdod, mentioned in Isaiah 20:1, has been dramatically illustrated by inscriptions on the walls of his palace. In 1963 an archaeological expedition at Ashdod, which included the author, found three fragments of a victory monument erected by Sargon's forces.

Archaeological discoveries help us understand obscure biblical words.—The value of archaeology has been increasingly important in language study. Much Greek writing on papyrus has been found in Egypt. Reading this shows that there is no essential difference between the Greek used in the New Testament itself and the ordinary Greek speech of the first century. This vernacular type of Greek is known as *Koine*, from a Greek word meaning "common."

The New Testament uses a number of words only once and others only two or three times. Such rarity of usage often creates a mystery as to exact meaning. For example, the Greek word *paidagōgos*, related to "pedagogue," is found only in 1 Corinthians 4:15 and Galatians 3:24–25. Martin Luther (1525) translated *paidagōgos* by a German word meaning "schoolmaster," directly influencing Tyndale's English version (1535). This, in turn, influenced the King James Version (1611), which reads: "Wherefore the law was our schoolmaster to bring us unto Christ" (Gal. 3:24). Luther had no way of knowing, of course, the precise meaning this term had when the New Testament was written. How much he misunderstood the passage in Galatians is seen when he wrote in his *Commentary*:

> Show me a pupil who loves his schoolmaster. How little love is lost upon them the Jews showed by their attitude toward Moses. They would have been glad to stone Moses to death (Exodus 17:4). You cannot expect anything else. How can a pupil love a teacher who frustrates his desires? And if the pupil disobeys, the schoolmaster whips him, and the pupil has to like it and even kiss the rod with which he was beaten. Do you think the schoolboy feels good about it? As soon as the teacher turns his back, the pupil breaks the rod and throws it in the fire. And if he were stronger than the teacher he would not take the beatings, but beat up the teacher.

Yet, in his Galatian letter, Paul is not actually saying that the Law is the teacher; he is saying that Christ is the Teacher! The *paidagōgos*, while having certain instructional duties, was primarily responsible as a "custodian" or "guardian." One papyrus text from a mother to her son, whose teacher (*kathēgētēs*) had just left him, gives instructions that he and his *paidagōgos* are to be on the lookout for another suitable teacher!

It is by archaeological research that this type of comparative literature is made available, helping to uncover the meaning of the biblical vocabulary.

2

The Method of Archaeology

▲▲▲

Like those of other scientists, modern archaeologists have developed their methods after many experiments of failure or success. Thus, the early history of archaeology shows many examples of wrong procedures and techniques. Unfortunately, much early work was carried on in the spirit of "treasure hunting." Unscrupulous adventurers, seeking precious objects which could be sold to the great museums, plundered Egyptian tombs and monuments. Early diggers in the ancient ruins of Mesopotamia carried on their activities with only one purpose in mind, and that purpose was to find archaeological loot.

Generally speaking, these pioneer diggers wasted no trouble nor time to record their discoveries. To a better informed generation, the accounts left by some of these early archaeologists read like legends about pirates.

For example, in 1853, H. Rassam excavated on the site of ancient Nineveh, capital city of the Assyrians. The French archaeologist V. Place also worked there at the same time. When Rassam observed that the French party was getting close to promising discoveries, he decided to use strategy. He worked at night in the area assigned to the French! In this manner, he "discovered" the library of Ashurbanipal, the Assyrian king mentioned in Ezra 4:10, and robbed his palace rooms of the impressive wall plaques which show him hunting lions. These treasures are today in the British Museum.

G. B. Belzoni (1778–1823), an Italian collector of antiquities, worked in Egypt in the early part of the nineteenth century. He provides a notorious example of atrocious methods. In fairness, it should be said that he (as well as Rassam) made some truly remarkable discoveries. Belzoni's work in 1817 called attention to the importance of the Valley of the Kings, near Thebes, where so many of the Egyptian pharaohs were buried. But his story of examining these tombs sounds like an account of vandalism. He frequently broke through the doors of tomb chambers with a battering-ram and trampled roughshod on whatever was in his path. He said:

> Every step I took I crushed a mummy in some part or other. . . . When my weight bore on the body of an Egyptian it crushed like a bandbox. I sank altogether among the broken mummies with a crash of bones, rags and wooden cases. . . . I could not avoid being covered with bones, legs, arms and heads rolling from above.

One shudders to read of such carelessness. These crude methods of plundering stand in utter contrast to the more careful techniques used by Howard Carter, for example, who discovered the tomb of King Tutankhamen in 1922. The world can be grateful that Carter, not Belzoni, found this tomb.

Thus, archaeology—like astronomy, which evolved from the crudities of astrology—has developed from a rather sinister past. The methods of archaeology, while still developing, call for some description at this point.

Definition and Purpose

The word "archaeology" is not a modern term. This term was used regularly by writers in the early period of the New Testament. Josephus, a Jewish historian who wrote in

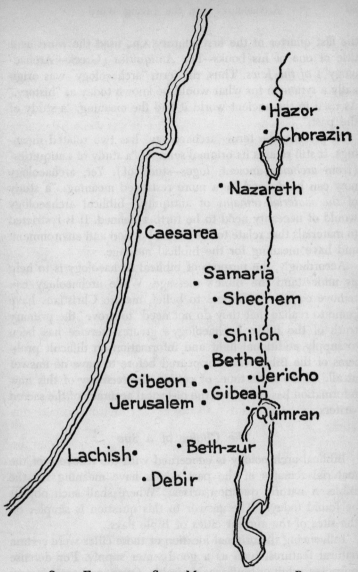

SOME EXCAVATION SITES MENTIONED IN THE BOOK

the last quarter of the first century A.D., used the word as a title of one of his books—*The Antiquities* (Greek—"Archaeology") *of the Jews*. Thus, the term "archaeology" was originally a synonym for what would be known today as "history." As used in the ancient world it had the meaning, "a study of the past."

At present, the term "archaeology" has two related meanings. It still retains its original sense of "a study of antiquities" (from *archaios*—ancient; *logos*—study of). Yet, archaeology now can be defined by a more restricted meaning: "a study of *the material remains* of antiquity." Biblical archaeology would of necessity need to be further defined. It is restricted to materials that relate to the biblical period and environment, and have meaning for the biblical message.

Accordingly, the purpose of biblical archaeology is to help us understand the Bible's message. While archaeology can remove certain hindrances to belief, mature Christians have come to realize that they do not need "to prove" the primary truth of the Bible. Archaeology's greatest service has been to supply additional light and information on difficult problems of the Bible which appeared before to have no answer at all. At the same time, of course, the recovery of this new information has confirmed the historical accuracy of the sacred writers.

The Choice of a Site

Biblical archaeology is concerned with the recovery of the material remains of the past which have meaning for the Bible. A natural question arises: "Where shall such objects be found today?" The answer to this question is simple: on the sites of the ancient cities of Bible days.

Influencing the original location of those cities were certain natural features, such as a good water supply. For defense purposes, a hill or bluff was desirable. Often, economic factors entered in. Towns sprang up along trade routes or near harbors. Thus, once they were settled, towns would be occupied for centuries.

Since a site was chosen for favorable natural features, it is easy to see why people would live there for thousands of years. Jericho supplies an excellent example. As far as can now be determined, it is one of the oldest settlements in the world. A British archaeologist, Miss Kathleen Kenyon, who excavated Jericho (its modern name is Tell es-Sultan) in 1952–58, discovered that the spot was well established by 7800 B.C. Some vestiges of occupation could be dated even earlier. Jericho was well located near an abundant spring. Agriculture was even sustained by irrigation from this bountiful source of water.

Over the millennia, the deposits left by Jericho's settlers caused the areas of habitation to grow higher and higher. The mound of Jericho rises today approximately seventy feet above virgin soil. Like a layer cake, the mounds of ancient towns gradually formed throughout the Near East. The archaeological name for one of these mounds is "tell," from an Arabic name meaning "ruin heap." Archaeologists, by careful procedures, are able to dig into these mounds and make them yield their secrets by studying the material objects which are found.

How do archaeologists choose the sites which they excavate? Many factors enter into a decision. Often, an accidental discovery will prompt excavation of a site. At Mari, on the middle Euphrates, where documents have been discovered which throw much light on the period of Abraham, Isaac, and Jacob, a Sumerian statuette was discovered on the surface of the ground. This important "find" prompted the excavators to work there. Ras Shamra is located on the Mediterranean coast south of Antioch. Here much written material has been discovered which tells of Canaanite religious beliefs.

The site was discovered by a farmer while plowing. Qumran, eight and a half miles south of Jericho, was the center of the Essene community that produced the Dead Sea Scrolls. It was excavated to see what relationship existed between its ruins and the scrolls which were accidentally discovered in nearby caves.

Archaeologists most often work at significant places which are referred to frequently in the Bible, such as Bethel, Jericho, Jerusalem, or Shechem. In any event, a mound must be accessible and a sufficient team of laborers must be close at hand to make excavation work possible.

Selection of a Staff

Trained workers are essential if reliable results are to be expected in an excavation. A staff usually can be divided into three groups: trained personnel, students or teachers who are seeking experience, and native workers. The first two groups normally receive no monetary compensation from expedition funds other than lodging, and in select cases, travel expenses. The native workers are local day-laborers who are hired at a fixed rate, according to the functions they are expected to perform: pickmen, hoemen, basketboys, pottery-washers, cooks, or otherwise.

The excavator himself must be a person of wide experience, leadership, and gifts. It is extremely important that he be able to get along with those who work with him. It is easy for tempers to flare and for patience to be short as a blistering sun beats down on a weary company of excavators. Firmness, mixed with fairness, toward the workers always brings greatest results. The workers available are often inexperienced and must be carefully supervised. Securing funds and setting aside time from regular work are additional problems restricting archaeological activity.

The Digging Process

Usually digs are carried on during the summer months, when the weather of the Near East is dry. Too, an archaeologist who teaches has lighter responsibilities at this time.

There is little uniformity of schedules. Each excavator usually tries to utilize the cool, early morning hours to the greatest advantage. For this reason, most digs begin at 5:00 A.M., if laborers are available and willing. The working staff eats a light breakfast of toast and jelly upon arising; then about 9:00 A.M. a regular breakfast may be served. Actual excavating continues until about 1:00 P.M. The remainder of the day is used for cleaning, studying, and recording the objects discovered. In unusual circumstances two shifts of workers may be necessary.

No two excavations are alike. Each dig will present distinct problems which must be overcome if the work is to yield fruitful results. Nevertheless, the basic procedures and safeguards of excavating are fairly standard.

First, a permit for excavating must be secured. Each country of the Near East has a government agency which grants permits and is responsible for the care and preservation of its ancient places. This permit will not be granted to any unqualified group, and there is a fee attached to its issuance. The fee varies with the different countries but averages close to a thousand dollars.

A survey is made of the site to be excavated. All landmarks of importance and contour lines are accurately drawn. Ideally, the finished surveyor's chart is checked for accuracy with an aerial photograph of the site. Important clues to the location of ancient ruins may show up on aerial photographs taken at various times of day. This knowledge will guide the archaeologist in choosing suitable areas to dig. The surveyor's chart gives information and direction to those recording discoveries, as well as aid in planning the areas to be excavated.

Photographs are made of an area before excavations begin. In archaeology, as well as in art, a "picture is worth a thousand words." Moreover, at each stage of the work, and particularly when important discoveries are made, the photographer should be busy. No discovery should be hastily lifted out of its context. Discoveries should be photographed *in situ* (in their natural position when discovered) before being removed for safe deposit and study.

An excavator must be constantly alert for ways to improve the efficiency of his workmen. Hired workers may tend to "drag their feet" on the job. This tendency must be brought under control by the excavator or he will "toil all day and take nothing." Normally, it is better to divide the workers into small, efficiently organized teams. This enables the area supervisors to have better control over the workers, especially when discoveries are made.

Many workers will be tempted to steal small objects they discover, with the intention of selling them to black-market dealers. For this reason it is better to promise a bonus to workers who make real discoveries. This will encourage them to work harder and will prevent valuable objects from falling into outside hands.

One danger must be avoided, however. If the bonus is too high, the workers will be tempted to "import" objects to the excavation site. This is known as "salting." An excavator must be alert to detect such action. A small seal, scarab (a beatle-shaped amulet), figurine, or coin which has lain in the ground for many centuries will usually supply certain clues which, to a trained eye, tell a story. Coins left in the ground for centuries develop a patina (a green coating on bronze objects) or will be surrounded by a fresh, sharp crust of earth. If this crust is worn down smoothly, the excavator will know that the workman who turned it in must have carried the object in his pocket. Some penalty should be attached for those who try to get by with such acts.

Objects found should not be placed on the edges of the areas which are being excavated. This is a common mistake, for seemingly, the edge is a safe, convenient, out-of-the-way place. But there is too much danger that a careless workman or visitor will accidentally knock such objects to the ground. All discoveries should be marked with a tag which tells the date, position in excavation area, depth, and so on. They then should be placed in a basket by themselves. Visitors should be warned to keep away from the edge of an excavation area at all times, lest it collapse when they stand on it.

Careful records are kept day by day. All pottery pieces discovered are saved, washed, and carefully studied, since archaeologists use them for dating purposes. Each area supervisor keeps a record book. It contains the names of the workmen, the basket numbers, and depth and area where each basket was found. It lists all small objects and the name of the workman responsible for the find. Such information is invaluable when the final report is written.

Archaeologists can date pottery according to shape, design, and texture. Remember that pottery styles change. Thus, the trained eye of an archaeologist can tell at a glance whether a pottery fragment was made in the time of Jesus, Jeremiah, or Abraham.

As the work of excavation proceeds, other workers should be recording, mending, reconstructing, and drawing the objects found. Oftentimes pottery objects which have been broken can be restored completely.

Archaeologists usually divide their excavation areas into small plots, about 15 or 17 feet square. Between these squares a narrow ridge (called a "balk") of earth is left untouched. Usually the squares are close together, giving an appearance something like a waffle, with ridges and depressions. The ridge (or "balk") which is left is important, since it shows the various levels which have been penetrated. This serves as a convenient reference point when measurements must be made to record objects and levels which have been discovered.

All the objects found in an excavation must be divided with the national government. Governments today usually claim objects of great worth, since it is reasoned that valuable pieces should stay in the place of their discovery. Until recently, archaeologists were permitted by the laws of many countries to keep half of their discoveries. By this system either the archaeologist or an official of the antiquities department divided the discoveries into two piles. In order to insure fairness, the other party would have choice of either pile. Needless to say, the piles were always divided equally by this method!

As the digging operation proceeds, the excavation area naturally becomes very deep. It is important to instruct those digging (the hoemen and pickmen) to make sure that the sides of all squares be kept perfectly vertical and, as far as possible, that the floors be kept horizontal. Workers have a tendency to let the sides slant inward like a bowl. If the sides are not kept vertical the area being excavated is greatly reduced.

Also, the floor should be worked on a straight level, as far as possible. This helps the archaeologist keep all objects discovered in their proper relation. He will be able to assign accurate dates to new and unknown objects by their relationship to those whose age can be determined. The key to scientific archaeology is this principle of dating objects by their relation to other objects in the same level.

For this reason, it is important that an archaeologist not dig lower than the floor level before he clears it entirely. All objects above the floor level—plaster, flagstone, or hard-packed earth—naturally date later than the time the floor level was laid. By the same logic, all objects underneath the floor level date from an earlier time. This follows the recognized law that the lower deposits are older. Thus, careful distinctions can be made in accurately ascribing various objects to their proper periods. At the same time, archaeologists discover which articles were used in specific cultural periods. Thus, the biblical references to these various objects become meaningful and clear.

A coin expert, called a "numismatist," is responsible for cleaning and classifying the coins discovered. Coins, which became common after the period of Alexander the Great, give archaeologists their most accurate sources of information for establishing the date of the levels which are uncovered. Many of these ancient coins have precise dates, which substantially reduces chronological error. Pottery, on the other hand, when used for dating, must be given a considerable margin for possible error (approximately fifty years). Pottery is found in much greater abundance than coins, of course, and is still the most common evidence archaeologists use in dating. All of the photographs and information gathered by archaeologists while digging at one spot are carefully studied and finally presented in publications and reports. This enables others to know of new discoveries and help in interpreting new information.

These are only a few of the principles which are observed by archaeologists as they seek to understand the Bible better. The work is demanding and difficult. There is certainly nothing glamorous about the sweat, toil, and sacrifices that make expeditions possible. What makes the men who have given their lives to this work return to the Holy Land again and again to participate in excavations? They know that archaeology has proved its worth.

3

The Exodus and Conquest

▲▲▲

There is hardly an Old Testament event which has been discussed more in recent years than the Exodus. The mainstream of current opinion on this question has fairly well accepted the date for the Exodus sometime between 1300 and 1250 B.C. Archaeological discoveries in particular have done much to establish this approximate time. For the sake of clarity, the names of some of the Egyptian pharaohs who reigned between 1600 and 1200 B.C. should be listed and their main achievements described, especially as they have relationship to the Bible and to Palestine.

Historical Summary of Egyptian Pharaohs

Amosis I (1570–1545 B.C.).—This pharaoh expelled the Hyksos, Asiatic groups who controlled Egypt between 1720 and 1570 B.C. The Hebrews had certain connections with the Hyksos. Amosis was likely the pharaoh who "knew not Joseph" (Ex. 1:8). Amosis I was the founder of the eighteenth dynasty, a ruling family which controlled Egypt for about 250 years (1570–1321 B.C.).

Thutmosis III (1490–1435 B.C.).—Under this pharaoh, Egypt rose to great heights of military grandeur and power. He carried out numerous military expeditions in Palestine and has been called the "Napoleon of ancient Egypt."

Akhenaten (1370–1353 B.C.).—This pharaoh was also called
Amenophis IV or Amen-Hotep IV. Born of an Asiatic mother
(Teye), he is famous as the monotheistic pharaoh who gave
supreme worship to the sun disk, Aten. He preferred to be
named after this god, Akhenaten meaning Splendor of Aten.
He moved the capital of Egypt from Thebes to his new
capital of Akhetaten. He neglected important governmental
matters; Egyptian power in the Asiatic districts (Palestine-
Syria) thereby declined. In A.D. 1887, several official documents, called the Tel el-Amarna letters, from the royal
archives of this pharaoh were discovered. These tablets mention the disorder and confusion which existed among the
Palestinian-Syrian areas under Egyptian control at this time.
Much of this disorder and trouble was caused by certain
bandit-type groups of people called "Hapiru" (Hebrews?)
who threatened to gain control of various territories in
Palestine.

Tutankhamen (1353–1344 B.C.).—This pharaoh was a son-in-
law of Akhenaten. He is today famous because of his tomb
discovery, made by Carter in 1922-23. Tutankhamen was a
weak king, comparatively speaking, since he died at the age
of 18.

Ramses I (1321–1320 B.C.?).—This pharaoh was the
founder of the nineteenth dynasty, though having but a short
reign. His family stemmed from Avaris, the old Hyksos capital,
and he was himself of Hyksos descent. He possibly made
some beginnings on constructing a new capital where Avaris
had been located, but could not have done much.

Sethos I (1320–1304 B.C.?).—This pharaoh began to re-
assert Egyptian control of Palestine. An inscribed victory
monument, bearing his name, has been discovered at Beth-
Shan, southwest of the Sea of Galilee. Sethos also worked on
the restoration of Avaris (this city was called Raamses [after
his son or father?]; cf. Ex. 1:11). It is probable that he was

the pharaoh who oppressed Israel (Ex. 1:9 ff.). An inscription
has been found which mentions that four hundred years
transpired between the expulsion of the Hyksos (1720 B.C.)
and the building of Raamses, his capital, which would mean
the work began around 1320 B.C.

Ramses II (1304–1237 B.C.).—This pharaoh is conjectured
to be the one who ruled Egypt during the time of the
Exodus. Perhaps this event occurred in the early period of his
long career. Ramses frequently found himself at war with
the Hittites for control of Syria-Palestine. Ramses II continued the work on the capital city which was begun by
his father.

This northern location of his capital gave him closer contact
with affairs on his frontiers. Ramses II had a long reign and
later pharaohs frequently expressed the hope that they would
be favored by the gods to reign as long as he did! Thus, his
son, Merneptah, was an old man when he came to office and
died after a few years.

Merneptah (1237–1229 B.C.).—It is most unlikely that the
date of the Exodus is to be placed after Merneptah, since this
pharaoh mentioned that in his fifth year (around 1232 B.C.),
during the course of a military campaign in Palestine, he
fought Israel. Thus, Israel must have been in Caanan by this
time. Merneptah boasted: "Plundered is Pekanan (Caanan)
with every evil, carried off is Ashkelon; seized upon is Gezer,
Yenoam is made as a thing not existing, Israel is desolated, his
seed is not."

Most authorities agree that the dates here given for most
of these various pharaohs are approximately correct within
a period of about a decade. In being considerate of other
views, it should be said that there have been many different
suggestions made for the time of the Exodus, of course. A
generation ago many writers favored a date for the Exodus
which would have placed this event around 1440 B.C. Recent

discoveries have given greater weight to the reconstructed outline as suggested above. Some of these discoveries will now be summarized briefly.

Glueck's Work in Transjordan and the Negev

Nelson Glueck, now president of the Hebrew Union College, Cincinnati, Ohio, was trained in archaeological method by the outstanding archaeologist W. F. Albright. Glueck, who has carried on several expeditions in the southern regions of Transjordan and Palestine, has studied carefully the over-all pattern of the periods of occupation in these areas. Here it should be pointed out that archaeologists do not always need to excavate to determine when sites were occupied. The times of settled occupation can be determined on the basis of the types and styles of pottery and other evidences which are found on the surface of the ground around a given spot. Glueck observed that the southern desert or Negev regions had a similar historical pattern and were occupied during the following periods:

(1) Late Chalcolithic (3500–3200 B.C.).—transition from use of stone to copper implements. (The "Bronze Age" in Palestine dates from 3200 to 1200 B.C., and the "Iron Age" from 1200 to 550 B.C. Numbers in listings below refer to subdivisions of these periods.)

(2) Middle Bronze I (2150–1900 B.C.; note a break of more than a thousand years from the previous period of occupation)—Glueck, whose view is questioned, places Abraham near the end of this period.

(3) Late Bronze II to Iron II (1300–586 B.C.).—occupation in Transjordan only at beginning, starting in southern Palestine around 900; terminated by conquests of Nebuchadnezzar.

(4) Nabatean (second century B.C.-A.D. 106)—most flourishing time.

(5) Roman (63 B.C.-A.D. 323).

(6) Byzantine (A.D. 323–636)—final occupation before civilization in area was destroyed during the Moslem conquests.

The Israelites, it will be remembered, encountered various settlements at the time of the Exodus in this region of Palestine, and particularly in Edom and Moab, which could not have had inhabitants before this date. For example, one of the stations of the Exodus was Punon (cf. Num. 33:42). Punon is known today as "Feinan." In examining this site, Glueck found that the pottery indicated that it was abandoned from 1900 to 1300 B.C. Around 1300 B.C., Punon was reoccupied with a settlement which lasted until Nebuchadnezzar's time. Understandably, this kind of evidence is very important for establishing the time before which the Exodus could not have occurred, just as the Merneptah Monument indicated the time before which it must have occurred (1232 B.C.). Glueck is convinced, therefore, that the Exodus could not have occurred before 1300 B.C.

The Mention of the City of Raamses (Ex. 1:11)

Although the personal name of the pharaoh who oppressed the Israelites is not given in the Bible, the names of the cities which the Israelites were forced to build (Pithom and Raamses) are mentioned. These cities were located in the northeast delta region of Egypt (see chart). Evidence which has come to light demonstrates that the early years of Ramses II were spent in intensive building activities in the city which bore his name, called "Raamses" in the Bible.

Archaeologists have identified the location of the city Raamses by inscriptions on pottery. An Egyptian archaeologist, M. Hamza, recently excavated a site which is today named Qantir. He discovered five inscribed pieces of pottery which mention the very name of Per-Ramses, which means "house of Ramses." Just twelve miles north of this place is San el-Hagar which was the location of Tanis, called "Avaris" in the Hyksos period (between 1720 and 1570 B.C.). Tanis was perhaps combined with Raamses; together they seem to have formed the large, spread-out capital city of Ramses II at this time.

Intensive excavations in this ancient region of Raamses have demonstrated that between the Hyksos expulsion (1570 B.C.), when the Hyksos capital of Avaris was located there, and shortly before 1300 B.C., this area was entirely abandoned! As mentioned, somewhere around 1320 B.C., this site was made the new capital of Egypt (possibly by Ramses I, the pharaoh who began the Nineteenth Dynasty). Both Sethos and Ramses II greatly enlarged and beautified this capital. The Bible describes the Israelites of the Exodus as participating in the construction of Raamses. Since its construction was not begun until around 1320, the Exodus can hardly be dated before this time!

Pithom seems to be accurately identified with a site which is today called Tell er-Retabeh (see map).

The Bible says the Israelites had to gather straw for the bricks to build the cities of Pithom and Raamses (cf. Ex. 5:7–18). It has been demonstrated scientifically, on the basis of experiments, that the kind of adobe bricks used at this period were three times stronger when they had such straw than they would be otherwise. This strength is due to a chemical reaction (humic acid) caused by the straw's decay in the brick.

Other evidences for dating the time of the Exodus between 1300 and 1275 B.C. will appear in the discussion of the cities of the Conquest mentioned below. The Merneptah Monument requires a date no later than 1232 B.C., for he fought with Israel as a people in western Palestine. To allow some time for the period of wilderness wanderings and for the conquest under Joshua seems only reasonable in light of the biblical statements to this effect. Probably therefore, the Exodus should be dated sometime in the early years of Ramses II, whose oppressive building operations caused the event to take place between the period of 1295–1275 B.C.

The Cities of the Conquest

The archaeological histories of many of the Old Testament sites, which the Bible mentions as being conquered by Joshua's

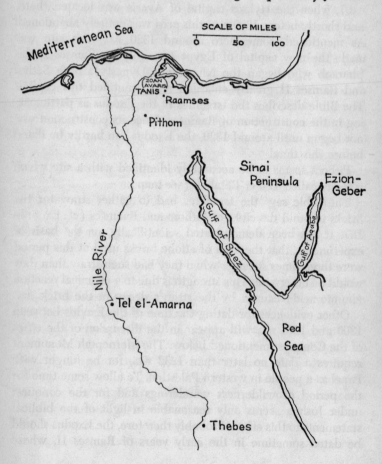

forces, fit well into the 1295–1275 B.C. date for the Exodus. Excavations have shown that the main wave of destruction for these Canaanite cities which were captured by Joshua occurred in approximately the last half of the thirteenth century (around 1250–1225 B.C.). Some of these excavations will be briefly reviewed here.

Hazor.—This site (located at the modern Tell el-Qedah) is famous as the place where Joshua's forces defeated a confederacy of Canaanite powers commanded by Jabin, the king of Hazor (see Josh. 11:1–14). Hazor is spoken of as the "head of all those kingdoms" (Josh. 11:10). The vast dimensions of territory of this site show that it was indeed a great city. The tell, combined with a large enclosure on the north, covered almost 180 acres and had room for at least forty thousand people. Recently discovered documents from Mari, dating somewhat before Joshua's time, imply that Hazor was the most significant place between the Euphrates and Egypt.

Hazor was located about ten miles due north of the Sea of Galilee. It was excavated by the British archaeologist John Garstang, in 1928, with inconclusive results. Beginning in 1955, the Jewish archaeologist Yigael Yadin carried on full-scale work there each season until 1959, with some minor excavations since then. A recent discovery of a Sumerian tablet at Hazor (found in 1963, and the only tablet of its kind ever found in Palestine!) is most interesting. It fits into other evidence which shows that the main mound at Hazor was well settled by 2800 B.C. From this time until its abandonment in the second century B.C., there were twenty-two stratified layers which have been discovered. Each layer, of course, represents an ancient city.

Garstang thought that Hazor was abandoned by the Canaanites as early as 1400 B.C. However, the later excavations under Yadin demonstrated conclusively that it was not until approximately 1250–1230 B.C. that the Canaanite city came to an end. The date of Hazor's destruction by Joshua is of the highest importance for establishing the time of the Exodus. So thoroughly did Joshua's forces destroy Hazor that the vast enclosure on the north (3600 by 2250 ft.) was never reoccupied, though its main mound (fifteen acres) was resettled by Israelites in the time of Solomon (see 1 Kings 9:15).

The Israelite attackers of Hazor showed great disdain for the religious objects of those conquered. This is evidenced by the way heads were knocked off the idols. Religious monuments of the Canaanite gods were thrown down in disordered heaps; other images of animals were thrown into pits. An interesting religious object which was found at Hazor seems to show that the Canaanites also had a practice of holding up a pole with a bronze plaque on it which depicted serpents, just as the Israelites did (see Num. 21:9). Three temples of the Canaanites were found at Hazor. The architectural plan of these temples resembled the plan of Solomon's Temple. This should not surprise us too much, however, since the Bible informs us that Canaanites (Phoenicians) built the Temple of Solomon (see 1 Kings 5:18).

Beth-zur.—Joshua 15:58 mentions that Beth-zur was occupied by the Israelites about the time of the Conquest. Beth-zur (called today Khirbat et-Tubeiqa) was excavated in 1931 and 1957. Excavations have shown that Beth-zur was intensively settled at approximately 1800 and 1600 B.C., roughly the Hyksos period. At this time, however, Beth-zur suffered a catastrophe and the town was destroyed. It was uninhabited for almost four hundred years. Sometime before 1200 B.C. the invading Israelites seem to have rebuilt this town.

Gibeon.—Gibeon is located six miles northwest of Jerusalem. Excavations there have been carried on by James B. Pritchard over four seasons (1956, 1957, 1959, 1960). His work has shown that Gibeon was first occupied around 2800 B.C., with almost steady occupation through the Roman period. It is still occupied and is called "el-Jib" today.

The early excavations of Pritchard, however, were very puzzling, since no evidence could be found that Gibeon was occupied in the period of Joshua (the Late Bronze Age, between 1550 and 1200 B.C.). It will be remembered that the Gibeonites were clever enough to avert destruction by Joshua's army by deceiving the Israelites (see Josh. 9:3–27). For this deception, Joshua made the Gibeonites "hewers of wood and drawers of water."

In 1960, Pritchard discovered the first evidence which could be dated around Joshua's time. In a cemetery on the west side of Gibeon he found a considerable amount of pottery in three Late Bronze Age tombs, which seem to date as late as the thirteenth century B.C.

Pritchard also found a large, circular stairwell (37 feet in diameter), cut through the living rock, which he suggested was the Pool of Gibeon, mentioned in the time of David (see 2 Sam. 2:13). Mention has already been made of the 27 inscribed jar handles recovered from this pool.

Debir.—This Canaanite town is probably to be located today at Tel Beit Mirsim. Debir, known as Kirjath-Sepher at an earlier time, was also one of the numerous towns the Bible mentions that was taken at the time of the Israelite conquest (see Josh. 10:38 ff.; 15:15–17; Judg. 1:11–13).

In 1926–32, W. F. Albright conducted four seasons of excavations at Debir. The archaeological researches there are very important, because of the excellent opportunity afforded to check the way successive civilizations so frequently rose and fell before and after the Conquest. The study of the remains at Debir have been important for showing the evolution of pottery in Palestine between 2300 and 587 B.C., since it was occupied almost continuously in this period.

Debir is located only ten miles southwest of Hebron and was situated in the open country with little protection from outside aggressors. The place was destroyed repeatedly but was rebuilt immediately each time. At the end of the Late

Bronze Age (around 1225–1200 B.C.), the city was destroyed by fire and resettled almost immediately. Likely the capture of the city at this time was by the Israelites, under Joshua, as indicated in the Bible passages cited above.

Lachish.—This site is known today as Tell ed-Duweir. It was excavated by James Starkey in 1933–38. (Starkey was murdered in 1938 while on his way to the dedication of the new Rockefeller Museum in Jerusalem.) Various evidences were found at the site that indicate that it was still under Egyptian control in the time of Ramses II. An inscribed fragment of pottery found there which mentioned a certain "year four" seems by the character of its script to date from the time of Merneptah. This fragment, called a "sherd" or "ostracon," has been interpreted as fixing the time of the fall of Lachish with great precision. The excavations seem to indicate that the city of Lachish fell shortly after Merneptah's fourth year; in other words, around 1232 B.C. This capture of the city of Lachish by the Israelites is described in Joshua 10:31 ff.

Other sites connected with the conquest of Joshua (e.g., Jericho and Ai) yield less positive conclusions for fixing the time of the Exodus as accurately as these which have just been discussed. Nevertheless, out of the numerous theories which have been offered for fixing the date of the Exodus, none satisfies the evidence so well as approximately 1295–75 B.C. The Conquest, on this theory, thus began approximately a generation thereafter (1250–35 B.C.).

4

The Religion of the Canaanites

▲▲▲

Finding a lost alphabet and gaining the key to its interpretation are among the most fascinating aspects of archaeological discoveries. During the long course of archaeology's march of progress several lost languages have been recovered and successfully deciphered.

For years the writings of the ancient Egyptians remained mysteries. The Egyptians used a complicated kind of picture-writing called "hieroglyphics." A more simplified style, the "hieratic," came in later, but neither of these could be read. In 1798, when Napoleon was in Egypt, some of his soldiers found an inscription which was written in these Egyptian characters and in Greek. This inscription, known as the Rosetta Stone, provided the key which finally led to the successful interpretation of the writings of the ancient Egyptians. In 1823, a Frenchman named Champollion finally deciphered the Rosetta Stone by comparing the Greek part of the inscription with the unknown parts.

In 1833, an Englishman named Rawlinson successfully deciphered one of the three languages (Persian) on another inscription of great importance—the Behistun Inscription. This inscription, which was cut into the rock on a high mountain in ancient Persia, was made originally by command of Darius the Great, an ancient king between 521 and 486 B.C. Rawlinson's work finally led to the successful deciphering of the unknown languages of the Elamites and Babylonians (Accadian), which were also inscribed on this monument. When lost languages can be interpreted again, new chapters in ancient history can be written.

Some languages, of course, have been turned up by archaeologists which have been very difficult to decipher. The ancient people of Crete had such languages. Sir Arthur Evans discovered puzzling clay tablets when he excavated in Crete over sixty years ago. One of these Cretan languages (now called Minoan Linear B) has been translated only in the last decade by the British architect Michael Ventris. In 1964, in Palestine, a Dutch archaeologist named Franken has discovered an unknown language on clay tablets which no one has been able to translate, though it is certainly Semitic and doubtless will soon be translated. Some believe this new language to be Philistine.

The ancient town of Ugarit was located north of the eastern shore of the Mediterranean Sea. The "finger of Cyprus," as it is called, seems to point directly to this town. In 1928, this ancient town (now abandoned and called Ras Shamra) was rediscovered by accident, though its original name Ugarit was not known at the time. As mentioned in an earlier chapter, a farmer discovered this place while plowing. A French team of archaeologists, upon investigation, discovered that before 1200 B.C. this town had been an important seaport, but it had been abandoned around the period of the Israelite conquest of Palestine. Because of the important discoveries which this place has yielded, French archaeologists continue to excavate there whenever possible.

A script, written on clay tablets, was discovered at Ugarit in 1929. When deciphered, it turned out to be a previously unknown form of Canaanite, a Semitic language. The Canaanites, as we now know, were directly related to the Phoenicians.

The Israelites, it will be remembered, overcame numerous groups of Canaanites when they began to conquer Palestine under Joshua.

The most interesting information derived from the Ugaritic documents, as they relate to the Bible, concerns the new knowledge which they supply about Canaanite religion. During the times of the Exodus and the Conquest, the Israelites were brought into direct contact with the gods of the Canaanites. Considerable influence on the Canaanite gods was already present in the delta region of Egypt, as well as in Moab during the sojourn of the Israelites in these places. But the struggle between the prophets of Israel and the prophets of Baal, one of the chief gods of the Canaanites, reached its climax during the time of Elijah in the famous encounter on Mount Carmel. This new information from the Ugaritic sources on Canaanite religious beliefs and practices helps immeasurably in understanding why the spiritual leaders of Israel's God, Yahweh, spoke out so boldly against Baal and all that was associated with his cult. The Ugaritic religious writings date from around 1400 B.C. but seem to contain many reflections that date to a period as early as 1800 B.C.

The Canaanite Gods

The names of the gods of the Canaanites (El, Baal, Dagan, and so on) are not as familiar to the modern world as those of the Greeks and Romans (Zeus, Mars, Hercules, Venus, and so on). Therefore, at this point the names and characters of these various Canaanite gods should be listed and briefly described.

El.—Originally thought of by the Canaanites as head of all their deities, El is called the "Father of Years." As head of the Canaanite family of gods (pantheon), he acted as judge to settle family disputes. By the time of the Old Testament writers El had been displaced long since by Baal. Baal was robust, virile, and caused the fields, as well as the cattle, to be fertile. El was growing old and senile, and was already in his dotage. "El" is the same word which is sometimes used in the Old Testament to refer to the God of the Jews. However, the Hebrew concept of God was quite different from that of the Canaanites.

Asherah (or Athirat).—This goddess is mentioned frequently in the Old Testament, but her name was mistranslated in the King James Version as "groves." She was the wife of El in the Ugaritic texts but, strangely, is frequently associated with Baal in the Old Testament (cf. Judg. 3:7; 1 Kings 18:19; 2 Chron. 33:3). Doubtless, the reason for this is the difference in the time between the Ugaritic period (1800 to 1400 B.C.) and the time of the prophets (1000–600 B.C.). By a gradual process, Baal (the son of El) replaced El as the husband of Asherah in the incestuous thought of the Canaanites! Obviously, this is in sharp contrast to the Hebrew thought of a God who was without sexual relationships of any kind.

Baal.—Baal is the main hero of the Ugaritic materials. The name "Baal" means possessor, owner, energizer, or, husband. Since he was also the lord of the storm, he had the alternate name of "Hadad," which means the thunderer. He was thought of as controlling the power of nature. It is easy to understand why the Israelites would be tempted to worship him. If they failed to do so, they feared that they might have crop failures. Therefore, to worship this god was a real temptation to the Israelites, who were settling down to an agricultural life after the Conquest.

Baal also controlled the fertility of animals and of people. His worship was very sensuous. Numerous cultic prostitutes were on duty at various worship centers, where they would serve the name of this god with their bodies. Many of these religious centers where Baal was worshiped, such as Baal-berith at Shechem, are mentioned in the Old Testament (see Judg. 8:33; 9:4).

Anath.—Anath was thought of as Baal's sister and consort in fleshly pleasures. When she mated with Baal, the cattle were made to bear their young by a process of sympathetic magic. When Baal was killed by his enemy Mot, the god of death, Anath avenged him by killing Mot. Anath was a very bloodthirsty goddess and also was in charge of animal hunts. Her name occurs in the Old Testament. Shamgar, one of the judges, is spoken of as "son of Anath" (cf. Judg. 3:31; 5:6). Various places were named in her honor; for example, Beth-anath or Temple of Anath in Naphtali (cf. Josh. 19:38); Beth-anoth in Judah (cf. Josh. 15:59); Anathoth (cf. Jer. 1:1; 11:21).

Astarte.—This goddess is referred to in the Old Testament as Ashtaroth (plural) or Ashtoreth (singular). In Judges 2:13, this goddess is spoken of as the counterpart of Baal: "They forsook the Lord, and served Baal and Ashtaroth." The Ugaritic texts also represent her in identical terms, since she is the goddess of love and fertility and is beloved by Baal. She also presided over battles in which her worshipers were engaged. It will be remembered that the Philistines, after the battle of Gilboa, dedicated the military spoils, which they had taken from Saul and Jonathan, to Astarte at her temple, which was located in the city of Beth-shan (cf. 1 Sam. 31:8–13).

Dagan.—Not only is El called the father of Baal in the Ugaritic texts, Dagan is also so designated. He was the lord of grain (this is the meaning of his name) and is also spoken of several times in the Old Testament. Dagan is mentioned (Dagon is a variant spelling) as the chief god of Ashdod (cf. 1 Sam. 5:1–7) and also had a temple at Gaza, where Sampson was made to grind the grain dedicated to this god (cf. Judg. 16:23).

Minor gods and goddesses.—There were many other deities in the Canaanite divine assembly. There was Shapash, the sun goddess. Unlike the Babylonian Shamash, a *male* sun god, the Canaanite people of Ugarit thought of a *female* sun goddess. Yarakh was the name of the moon god; the city of Jericho was named in his honor.

Ashtar was the god of irrigation. He may be alluded to in the Bible under the figure of the "son of the morning" (cf. Isa. 14:12), who is not able to ascend to heaven but must be brought down to earth. In this portion of Isaiah, perhaps the writer's figure of speech is colored by pagan thought forms, since he is rebuking the pagans for their pride. Ashtar, according to a Canaanite text, after Baal's death tried to take over his throne! The *Baal Epic* informs us that Ashtar was expected to keep crops alive since Baal was dead. But Ashtar was too weak and small; thus, he was not able to carry on the work of Baal and was forced to vacate his throne.

> Replied Lady Asherah of the Sea:
>> "Well, let's make it Ashtar the Tyrant;
>> Let Ashtar the Tyrant be king."—
> Straightway Ashtar the Tyrant
>> Goes up to the *Fastness* of Zaphon
>> (And) sits on Baal Puissant's throne.
> (But) his feet reach not down to the footstool,
> Nor his head reaches up to the top.
> So Ashtar the Tyrant declares:
>> "I'll not reign in Zaphon's *Fastness!*"
> Down goes Ashtar the Tyrant,
>> Down from the throne of Baal Puissant,
>> And reigns in El's Earth, all of it.[1]

This portion of Isaiah applies this well-known story. Babylon had tried to rule the world (cf. Isa. 14:4), but, like Ashtar, was too weak for such a mighty undertaking and had to vacate the throne of world dominion.

There was also a divine craftsman (Kothar and Khasis) and an underworld deity named Mot, the god of death. There

---

[1] From J. B. Pritchard, *Ancient Near Eastern Texts* (Princeton: Princeton University Press, 1955), p. 140.

was likewise a god of the sea named Yam. His helper was a dragon of the sea named Lotan, which can be equated with the biblical "Leviathan." Mot and Yam were enemies of Baal and fought with him on various occasions.

Elijah's Contest with the Baal Prophets

Carmel, which means a "garden land" or "vineyard," is one of the most lovely mountain ranges in Palestine. It is eighteen hundred feet high and spreads out to the south and to the southeast for twelve to fifteen miles. Much rainfall and dew make the range a choice area for the production of crops, especially grapes for the making of wine.

The sacred area devoted to Baal on Mount Carmel probably dated from a very early time. Mount Carmel is called the "Sacred Cape" in Egyptian documents, which date from the time of Thuthmosis III (after 1490 B.C.). At any rate, here the contest between Elijah and the prophets of Baal took place.

The contest came in the early years of Ahab. We know from Assyrian sources that Ahab died about the year 853 B.C. Since the Bible says that he reigned twenty-two years (cf. 1 Kings 16:29), Ahab must have become king around 875/874 B.C. Therefore, this event probably dates around 870 B.C.

The conflict between the religion of Baal and the religion of Yahweh, the God of the Israelites, was intensified at this time. Jezebel, Ahab's wife, waged an intensive campaign to uproot Yahwistic influence within her borders. She even had all religious altars to Yahweh torn down. Her zeal for Baal worship is partly explained by the fact that her father Ittobaal (whose name means "Baal is with you") was at this time not only King of Tyre but also high priest of the temple of Astarte.

Information is limited about the four hundred prophets of Asherah, who were supported by royal patronage (see 1 Kings 18:19). In 1902–3, an archaeologist named Sellin found at

Taanach (see Judg. 5:19), near Megiddo, various clay tablets which contained the mysterious statement, "If the finger of Asherah points. . . ." Probably oracles were given in the name of the goddess and her prophets interpreted them to inquirers, particularly to members of the royal family.

Much more knowledge is available on the prophets of Baal whom Elijah refuted. The particular Baal who was served by these prophets had a special connection with Tyre, just as Asherah did. This Baal of Tyre is to be identified with Melkart, who was also known to the Greeks as Herakles.

Elijah's ridicule of the prophets of Baal is one of the most vivid descriptions of a specific situation in the Old Testament. Every point in which he mocks Baal as powerless to help his prophets can be illustrated by archaeological and literary evidence. In the words of Skinner, Elijah was "the greatest religious personality that had been raised up in Israel since Moses." Yet, of all the events in Elijah's life, he shows himself at his greatest in this blistering exposure of Baal religion and in his matchless faith in the power of the living God. The remarkable thing about the Elijah episode is that the prophets of Baal did not cut Elijah to pieces with the same knives with which they gashed themselves! Elijah's sarcasm was as demolishing to their position as the fire from heaven: "Cry aloud, for he is a god; either he is musing, or he is gone aside, or he is on a journey, or perhaps he is asleep and must be awakened" (1 Kings 18:27, RSV).

The prophets of Baal were now at their wits' end. The contest had been agreed upon as a method of deciding who was the true God. The main issue of the contest was that the god who was able to kindle the sacrifice was to be thought of as the god who was able to give the rain. This issue is understood more clearly when it is realized that ancient monuments frequently depict Baal with a lightning bolt in his hand. Baal's prophets urged him to hurl his lightning bolts and thus consume this sacrifice which they had prepared for him.

"They limped about the altar." These words indicate that the prophets of Baal performed a characteristic dance. Heliodorus, a Syrian writer who lived around the third century A.D., described a dance performed by sailors of Tyre in honor of their god Herakles (Baal-Melkart). His description fits exactly the limping action of the Baal prophets of Elijah's time: "All of them leap in the air with nimbleness, all of them bend their knees near the ground, and revolve around each other like they are possessed" (*Aethiopica* IV.XVII.1).

Cumont has called attention to an artistic relief which depicts such ecstatic dancers. The dancers are represented as being in a frenzy. They make various contortions with their bodies, have bent legs, and various spectators are shown clapping their hands while the dancers perform. It will be remembered that God told Elijah that seven thousand Israelites had not "bent their knees" (1 Kings 19:18) by engaging in this kind of dancing, which was characteristic of those who worshiped Baal.

"He is musing." This reference is probably to be understood as a reference to the Baal of Tyre as a philosophical, meditative deity. The idea is that this god was occupied with his own thoughts and was deep in meditation. Therefore, he was unable to help these prophets who frantically called upon him. Melkart was sometimes called the "philosopher" and was credited with the invention of shipping.

"He is on a journey." In the Ugaritic legends these are frequent references to various journeys which Baal was required to make—to a northern mountain (Zaphon), to the underworld, and so on. By the time of Elijah there were other legends that Baal made journeys to Libya and frequently visited Tyrian colonies, as far away as Spain and Gibraltar. The early coins of Tyre show Melkart riding on a seahorse or dolphin. Thus, it is easy to see why Elijah refers to Baal as

a faraway tourist who was more interested in distant places than in his prophets!

"He is asleep." In the Ugaritic myths, Baal is represented as being killed by Mot. Baal died for seven years, and since he was the god of fertility all vegetation likewise perished on the earth for seven years. In the same documents, Baal was hesitant to permit the divine craftsmen, Kothar and Khasis, to build him a house, that is a temple, without a window since he feared that the god of death would come through the window to bring harm to him while he was asleep. Likely, other legends gradually grew up which represented Baal as sleeping.

Josephus (*Antiquities* VIII.v.3) speaks about a certain festival which was kept in the spring by the people of Tyre to awaken Herakles from his winter sleep. In the thought of other religions of this period, mention is made of a daily service held each morning in pagan temples in which the gods would be awakened. For example, the ancient Egyptian priests in the time of Elijah would chant a ritual which would be directed to their gods to "awake in peace."

"They cried aloud and cut themselves." Such behavior was typical of other religions in Syria and the Near East at the time. Oftentimes, priests worked themselves up into such a frenzy that they actually deprived themselves of their reproductive powers.

Against the background of all of these excesses, the faith of Elijah stands in utter contrast. There was only one true God in Elijah's thought. The idea of a multiplicity of gods—Baal, Asherah, Astarte, and so on—was not a concept with which Elijah could find sympathy. The wild excesses, sex, and prostitution which were associated with Baal religion were utterly contemptible to him and to all true prophets of God.

Instead of the mythology and magic which were found in the Baal cult, the faith of Israel was based on the action of

God in history. The fire which fell when Elijah refuted these Baal prophets became itself a new manifestation of God's power. This helped to quicken and to inspire the faith of Israel in a living God who did not slumber or sleep (cf. Psalm 121:4).

5

Ancient Law Codes

▲▲▲

The first ancient documents containing civil laws which strongly resembled those of Moses were found as early as 1853. Rassam found a few clay tablets which contained ancient legislative materials when he excavated Ashurbanipal's library at Nineveh. It was many years, however, before these tablets were identified accurately. At first it was believed that Ashurbanipal (who died about 626 B.C.) must have been responsible for the formulation of the laws represented by the tablets, since they were found in his library. For a while, therefore, these laws were called the "Code of Ashurbanipal." We now know that Ashurbanipal was greatly interested in older literature and authorized his scribes to collect for his personal library not only ancient laws but numerous other writings from the past.

In 1901, a German named Delitzsch suggested that the legal documents found by Rassam were much older than the time of Ashurbanipal and must have been written originally by Hammurabi, a famous king of Babylonia (1728-1686) B.C.). At the same time, archaeologists who were working far away from Delitzsch found a conical pillar (in three fragments which fit together perfectly), which contained a copy of Hammurabi's laws! This proved that Delitzsch was right. The laws of the tablets matched the more complete laws on the pillar.

The Laws of Hammurabi

The more complete Code of Hammurabi was found at Susa by J. de Morgan, a French archaeologist. This monument shows Hammurabi, with right hand raised, swearing to Shamash, the sun-god, who was also regarded as the god of justice. The sun-god extends to Hammurabi a measuring rod and a large ring which resembles a bracelet, probably a rolled-up measuring line. These emblems show that Hammurabi was to promote justice and enforce accurate weights, measurements of land, and so forth.

Hammurabi's Code contains both an introduction and a closing statement. The introduction describes Hammurabi as a "wise shepherd" whom the gods Anum and Enlil appointed to "promote the welfare of the people" by preventing the strong from exploiting the weak. The closing statement mentions that Hammurabi was to deal justice to the orphan and widow and states that this was his reason for "writing my precious words" on his monument.

Originally the monument of Hammurabi's Code of law must have contained approximately 280 separate sections of law. At present there are 240 laws preserved on the monument since some erasure of lines has occurred. Missing sections can be restored in part by other tablets, such as those which Rassam found.

When Hammurabi's laws were first found, they created an electrifying, world-wide sensation because of their novelty. Now we know that Hammurabi was by no means the first to codify a body of laws. An ancient Sumerian king of the city of Lagash, who was named Urukagina, declared around 2400 B.C. that "he has established the ordinances of former times." One of his laws forbade wives to have more than one husband. A later king of Ur (Ur-Nammu, ca. 2060 B.C.) records that "according to the righteous laws of Shamash he made . . . justice to prevail." Shamash, as just seen, is represented as Hammurabi's patron god of law. Thus, the same gods are thought of as helping various kings of the Near East to formulate laws. The biblical laws themselves are very similar to many of these law codes.

The following list illustrates a few of the similarities (plus noticeable differences) between Hammurabi's Code and Old Testament legislation:

"If a son has struck his father, they shall cut off his hand" (Hammurabi 195).

"He that smiteth his father, or his mother, shall be surely put to death" (Ex. 21:15).

"If a man [of the rank of citizen] struck another citizen's daughter and has caused her to have a miscarriage, he shall pay 10 shekels for her miscarriage. If that woman has died, they shall put his daughter to death" (Hammurabi 209–10).

"When men strive together, and hurt a woman with child, so that there is a miscarriage, and yet no harm follows, the one who hurt her shall be fined, according as the woman's husband shall lay upon him; and he shall pay as the judges determine. If any harm follows, then you shall give life for life" (Ex. 21:22–23, RSV).

"If a citizen has destroyed the eye of a member of the aristocracy they shall destroy his eye. If he has broken another citizen's bone (or "tooth" [200]), they shall break his bone (or "knock out his tooth"). If he has destroyed the eye of a commoner or broken the bone of a commoner [who is inferior to his rank], he shall pay one mina of silver" (Hammurabi 196–198).

"If any harm follows, then you shall give life for life, eye for eye, tooth for tooth, hand for hand, foot for foot, burn for burn, wound for wound, stripe for stripe" (Ex. 21:23–25, RSV).

"If a citizen made a breach in a house, they shall put him to death in front of that breach and wall him in. If a citizen committed robbery and has been caught, that citizen shall be put to death" (Hammurabi 21–22).

"If a thief is found breaking in, and is struck so that he dies, there shall be no bloodguilt for him" (Ex. 22:2 RSV).

Hammurabi's Code relates to a great variety of legal matters—property, rents, duties of married couples to one another, duties of masters and slaves, murder, theft, slander, purchases (it was necessary to have a bill of sale to authenticate each purchase), kidnapping, interest rates, inheritance, wages and prices, adoption, and so on. Even though the code, as it is preserved, is voluminous, it is to be considered only a partial statement of the law as it existed in Hammurabi's time. Several copies of the code were on display in conspicuous places throughout Hammurabi's vast domain to inform his people of their rights before the law.

Since 1901, many other prebiblical law codes, some very fragmentary, have come to light. In 1915, A. T. Clay published a tablet which contained various Sumerian laws of a time before Hammurabi. Numerous other laws have also been found which date after Hammurabi's time.

The Code of Lipit-Ishtar

In 1919, H. F. Lutz copied three ancient tablets which belonged to a law code of Lipit-Ishtar. This man was a Sumerian king who lived 150 years before Hammurabi, since Lipit-Ishtar was king of Isin from 1868 to 1857 B.C. The clay tablets containing Lipit-Ishtar's Code were first found by an American archaeologist named J. P. Peters, who discovered them at Nippur, in southern Mesopotamia, around A.D. 1889–90. However, no one recognized the true significance of the tablets published by Lutz until 1947. In this year Francis R. Steele, of the University of Pennsylvania, translated and soon published four other newly-recognized fragments of the same law code. In this new material the name of Lipit-Ishtar occurred, which showed that he was the king who codified these ancient laws.

Lipit-Ishtar, like Hammurabi, also gives an introduction to his laws. He likewise calls himself a "wise shepherd" whom Anu and Enlil appointed to office to bring justice and safety to his people. In his closing word Lipit-Ishtar calls down a curse on transgressors of his laws or on any who would change his laws. Originally, Lipit-Ishtar's laws were also displayed in public on a "pedestal," as indicated in the clay copy now preserved.

Thirty-eight laws are now preserved from Lipit-Ishtar's Code. These laws deal with the same wide variety of subjects as Hammurabi's Code. One provision (number 9) states that if a person is caught in the orchard of his neighbor, he is subject to a fine of ten silver shekels. Another section sounds very up-to-date. It provides that if a landowner refuses to pay his taxes for three years, he shall forfeit his land to the individual who is willing to pay the back taxes (number 18). If a man rents an ox and injures it, he is subject to a fine. He must pay one-third of the animal's value if he injures its nose; one-half if he injures its eye; one-fourth if he breaks the horn of the animal or its tail (numbers 34–37).

The Laws of Eshnunna

From 1945 to 1949, an obscure mound known today as Tell Abu Harmal, which is located near the southern outskirts of modern Baghdad, was excavated. This work was directed by S. T. Baqir, who at that time was curator of the Iraq Museum. He found two tablets (one in 1945; the other in 1948) which constituted part of an ancient code of the laws of an unidentified king over the ancient kingdom of Eshnunna, located about seventy miles northeast of Babylon. These documents were later studied and published by Albrecht Goetze of Yale University.

This code, which is called "Laws of Eshnunna," comes before that of Hammurabi by several decades, dating somewhere around 1900 B.C. The code is written in a Semitic language known as Old Babylonian. The arrangment of the laws is again quite similar to Hammurabi's Code. It has an introduction, poorly preserved, which mentions that the god Enlil bestowed power on the kings of Eshnunna. There are preserved sixty laws which deal with wages and prices (which were already "fixed" at this early period!), contracts, interest, engagement and marriage, slaves, bodily injury, divorce, and so on. About three-fourths of these laws are very similar to Hammurabi's Code. Instead of the rigid law of retribution working as it did in most circumstances (eye for eye, foot for foot, and so on), the Laws of Eshnunna referred cases involving death to the king (number 48).

In some ways the Old Testament laws were more strict than Hammurabi or Eshnunna's codes, as seen in the following comparison:

But if the ox has been accustomed to gore in the past, and its owner has been warned but has not kept it in, and it kills a man or a woman, the ox shall be stoned, and its owner also shall be put to death (Ex. 21:29, RSV).

If an ox is known to gore habitually and the authorities have forewarned its owner, but he did not have his ox dehorned(?), if it gores a man and causes his death, then the owner of the ox shall pay two thirds of a mina of silver [one mina = 60 shekels] (Laws of Eshnunna, number 54).

If the ox of a man is known to gore habitually and the authorities have forewarned him, but he did not blunt its horns (and) did not pen it up, if it gores a man and causes his death, he shall pay half a mina of silver [one mina = 60 shekels] (Code of Hammurabi, number 251).

Careful examination of Eshnunna and Hammurabi's codes will reveal that the law of retribution was not applied as carefully as it was among the Israelites. These other laws favored the upper classes and the wealthy insofar as a money

fine enabled transgressors to escape the penalty of strict
retribution. Jesus took another step beyond Moses when he
warned against retaliation (see Matt. 5:38–48). At the same
time, we must realize that it was a concern for true justice
which led the ancient Jews to adopt the principle of strict
retaliation. The law of the Old Testament took seriously the
principle that the poor should not be at a disadvantage in
court.

The Law Code of Ur-Nammu

The laws of Ur-Nammu were discovered in 1952 by an
American. S. N. Kramer was in Istanbul, Turkey, studying
ancient tablets at the Museum of the Ancient Orient. A former curator wrote him about a tablet on deposit there which
contained "Sumerian laws." Since tablets of this kind are very
rare, Kramer's curiosity was immediately aroused. Through
the directions of his friend's letter, he did find the tablet and
proceeded to study it. After several days he was able to make
sense out of the document. He had discovered the earliest
law code known thus far!

Kramer deciphered the tablet which had originated with
Ur-Nammu, an ancient king of Ur who reigned around 2060
B.C. This law code again shows the striking persistency of the
form of these legal proclamations between 2100 and 1600 B.C.
It had an introduction in which Ur-Nammu was designated
by divine choice to establish justice in his land. According to
his report, when he came to office oppression and "chiseling"
were rampant. Ur-Nammu felt it his duty to protect orphans,
widows, and the helpless. He took it upon himself to see that
"the man of one shekel did not fall prey to the man of one
mina" [60 shekels]. There followed, just as we have seen in
Hammurabi's Code, a list of specific laws which Ur-Nammu
enforced.

At present, only five laws can be read with any clarity on

Ur-Nammu's tablet. These laws relate to trial procedures (by water ordeal); returning slaves to their owners; orchards and irrigation. The most interesting laws deal with fines connected with personal injuries: if a foot is cut off, ten shekels are to be paid by the offender; if a bone is severed (in the arm (?) or side), sixty shekels are to be paid; forty shekels are due if the nose is cut off. Ur-Nammu thus permitted a money fine in place of strict retribution.

The Hittite Laws

The Hittite Law Code was discovered by a German excavator, Hugo Winckler, who worked in 1906–12 at Boghaz-Köi in central Turkey. Boghaz-Köi was known as Hattusas in the period of the Hittites and served as their capital. These laws were first translated successfully in 1922 by a Czech linguist named F. Hrozný. During Winckler's excavations at Boghaz-Köi, he found approximately thirteen thousand whole or partially damaged Hittite tablets. Before his excavations, the Hittites were a people almost entirely unknown except for a few Egyptian and Old Testament references. The written sources of the Hittites recovered by Winckler provided the necessary records for knowing their history and laws.

The Hittite laws are divided into two hundred sections. The title, "If Anyone," is appropriate, since each law states what the penalty is "if a man" does thus and so. The Hittite laws, particularly as they contrast to the Assyrian Code, were quite lenient. Usually a penalty could be paid off in money.

A specific Hittite law helps us to understand Abraham's purchase of a plot of burial ground from Ephron the Hittite (see Gen. 23:3–20). Hittite law (see no. 46 ff.) imposed certain feudal obligations (such as providing soldiers in the event of war) upon landowners. However, one who purchased only a small portion of a larger field was not forced to assume these legal obligations. It is easy, therefore, to understand

Abraham's desire to purchase only the cave at the edge of Ephron's field (cf. Gen. 23:9) and his reluctance to acquire the whole field, in light of the law prevailing at the place where he was then residing.

While the Hittite Code, which dates around 1400 B.C., is somewhat later than Hammurabi's, it nevertheless has great value for the person interested in the Old Testament. Hittite laws grew even more lenient with the passing of time.

The Assyrian Code

The Assyrian laws were discovered in 1903–14, by a German expedition which worked at Ashur, the old capital of the Assyrians. These laws are roughly contemporaneous with the Hittite Code and date between 1500 and 1200 B.C.

The Assyrian laws impress modern readers as very severe, although there seems to be a definite attempt in them to be fair so that only the guilty are punished. Some of the laws are shocking! If a man flirts with another's wife and touches her, his finger is to be cut off; if he kisses her, his lips are to be cut off (number 9). This law assumes that children are married at the age of 10 (number 43). A man who slanders a woman's reputation is to be flogged forty times, assigned to work on the road one month, and is also castrated and forced to pay a mina [60 shekels] of lead (number 18).

New documents are being found continuously which provide rich insights into the laws which prevailed during the period of the Old Testament. The New Testament is also richly illuminated by the laws which governed the Greco-Roman world.

6

Old Testament Places and Personalities

Archaeology sometimes provides more information than the Bible itself about places or persons named in the Bible. Nevertheless, these places or persons are important primarily because the Bible mentions them.

Shiloh

Shiloh, where the tabernacle was located after the Israelites settled in the land of Canaan (cf. Josh. 18:1), is today called "Seilun." The Dead Sea Scrolls inform us that it was occupied in Jesus' time, but there were various periods when it was *not* occupied. These periods of abandonment are important for the light they shed on the Bible.

Shiloh was excavated in 1926, 1929, and 1932 by a Danish expedition directed by Hans Kjaer, with W. F. Albright as the archaeological advisor. The excavations have demonstrated that from 2000 until shortly before 1200 B.C., roughly the time of Joshua, Shiloh was unoccupied. It was then settled from about 1200 to 1050 B.C., when it was destroyed violently. Shiloh was then abandoned until the end of the neo-Babylonian Empire (540 B.C.), when it was occupied again, probably by people returning from Babylonian exile. All this helps us understand Jeremiah's prophecy that the Temple of his day would be destroyed: "Therefore will I do unto this house [the Temple in Jerusalem] . . . as I have done to Shiloh" (Jer. 7:14).

The Old Testament does not inform us that the Philistines destroyed Shiloh when they captured the ark which normally resided there (see 1 Sam. 4:1 ff.). Excavations, on the other hand, strongly indicate that Shiloh must also have been destroyed at approximately the same time that the ark of the covenant was captured. This fact helps us to understand Jeremiah's reference to this place.

Gibeah—Saul's Ancient Capital

Gibeah is today called Tel el-Ful, an Arabic name which means "the mound of beans." The Hebrew name "Gibeah" means "high place." This is due to the fact that it is 2,754 feet above sea level. Albright excavated there in 1922–23 and in 1933. In 1964, James Kelso and Paul Lapp carried on another season of excavation. The 1964 season largely confirmed the accuracy of Albright's earlier work, even though much progress has been made in archaeological techniques in recent years.

Albright discovered a simple, fortified citadel which seems to have been the very palace of Saul himself. Besides having defense towers for security, there was a modest living room, approximately 14 by 23 feet in size. Probably this was the very room where David played his harp for Saul's entertainment. The household pottery of Saul's palace was very plain, and was all of local, simple design. Also discovered in these excavations was a plow point—the earliest iron object known among the Israelites. Evidently, the manufacture of iron began about this time.

Ezion-geber—Solomon's Seaport

Ezion-geber is today called Tell el-Kheleifeh. In 1934, a German explorer, Fritz Frank, identified Ezion-geber as Solomon's shipping center (see 1 Kings 9:26–28; 10:11,22). It is located on the northern end of the Gulf of Aqabah. Some time after 1938, Nelson Glueck, discovered there a copper and iron foundry, which was used by Solomon's workmen to produce ingots that could be used for trading purposes. This port linked Palestine with India, Arabia, and Africa via the Red Sea. First Kings 10:22 tells us that Solomon had a "Tarshish" fleet. The word "Tarshish" means smelter. Glueck's excavations have thus helped us to understand what kind of trade products Solomon's fleet carried in exchange for the spices, gold, ivory, and so on, mentioned in the biblical references cited above. A later Judean king named Uzziah reactivated this smelter and constructed a wall around it. He even tried to copy Solomon's successful trading techniques by sending out a similar fleet, but it was wrecked by a storm (cf. 1 Kings 22:48).

The site of Ezion-geber was ideal for a smelter for other reasons. There are strong drafts of wind which blow continuously from the north. These winds seemingly enabled the flues on the smelter to function properly. There are rich mineral deposits of copper in the hills a few miles to the north of Ezion-geber. Information from the Bible about these deposits led to their recent rediscovery. A modern copper factory is located in this same general region today (at Timna), fifteen miles north of Ezion-geber.

Samaria—Capital of the Northern Kingdom

Samaria is located approximately fifty miles north of Jerusalem. It has been excavated by two teams of archaeologists: a Harvard expedition composed of D. G. Lyons (a graduate of Southern Baptist Theological Seminary), G. A. Reisner, and C. S. Fisher, 1908–10; J. W. Crowfoot, E. L. Sukenik, Miss Kathleen Kenyon, and C. S. Fisher, 1931–33, 35.

At the time Samaria was established as the Israelite capital it was an unoccupied site (cf. 1 Kings 16:24). A few stray shards were found from an earlier period (dated around 3000 B.C.), which indicated some sporadic occupation was at Samaria in remote antiquity. No sizable settlement was there before Omri had Samaria constructed as his new capital, around 880 B.C. The older capital of Israel was at Tirzah, which was relatively isolated and poorly oriented (see 1 Kings 14:17). Samaria was well situated with respect to Phoenicia, Egypt, and the coastal plain, and no doubt this is why Omri chose it for his new capital.

Archaeological discoveries at Samaria have been rich and of special importance. The early Israelite kings built their city in an elaborate style. Their masonry is unexcelled, for they used the finest dressed stones in buildings and the defense wall. The furnishings were also highly artistic, having beautiful inlay work made with pieces of decorated ivory. Amos doubtless had such furnishings in mind when he spoke about the ivory palaces" (cf. 3:15; 6:4; and 1 Kings 22:39). In the courtyard of the royal palace there was discovered a pool with a sloping access ramp on one of its sides. It is possible that this was the very pool where Ahab's bloodstained chariot was cleansed after the battle of Ramoth-gilead (cf. 1 Kings 22:38).

The pottery of Samaria at this time is also of superb quality. Shards of inscribed pottery found near Samaria give us examples of how Hebrew writing looked in the time of Amos and Jeroboam II (early eighth century B.C.).

Both teams of excavators found shards on which were written words in ancient Hebrew. Fragments of pottery were used quite commonly in Old Testament times as cheap writing materials. These potsherds served as duplicate records for tax payments from the surrounding districts to the palace of the king. They are of great value in the knowledge they give about the language, religion, and economic conditions in Israel at this time.

Bethel—Jeroboam's Religious Sanctuary

Known today as "Beitin," Bethel is located approximately eleven miles north of Jerusalem. W. F. Albright excavated here in 1927 and 1934; James Kelso, in 1954, 1957, 1960, and 1962. Bethel was inhabited in the Roman period and was captured by Vespasian around A.D. 68–9. Much of the site is still occupied, which prevents full-scale excavation.

Bethel is mentioned in the Old Testament sixty-five times, more than any other city except Jerusalem. During the period of the divided monarchy (930 to 587 B.C.), this place was indeed separate from the southern kingdom (of Judah). This can be determined by the absence of typical "royal jar handles." These are found at cities of this period that were under control of the Judean kings of David's line.

All excavations carried out at Bethel have searched for the famous temple where Jeroboam's "golden bull" was worshiped (see 1 Kings 12:28 ff.). Probably the bull (not "calf") was thought of as a pedestal supporting Yahweh, the God of the Jews, who stood upon it. Thus far, no trace has been found of Jeroboam's temple, though an interesting discovery has been made which relates to it. In the 1957 campaign a seal, which was written in South Arabic, was discovered, which dates from about the Solomonic period. It has been conjectured that it was used to seal bags of frankincense which were brought by caravans from South Arabia ("Sheba" in the Old Testament), perhaps for use in Jeroboam's sanctuary.

Jerusalem—Capital of the Southern Kingdom

Jerusalem is mentioned about 800 times in the Bible. The city was named in honor of Shalem, a Canaanite deity. The name "Jerusalem" means foundation of Shalem. Recent excavations by Kathleen Kenyon show that Jerusalem has been inhabited since its establishment long before 3000 B.C. As far as the archaeological evidence indicates, therefore, Jerusalem, not Damascus nor Byblos, is the oldest known city to be continuously inhabited.

Not only does archaeological evidence confirm that Jerusalem was inhabited as early as Abraham; Jerusalem is also referred to in Egyptian literary documents (known as the "Execration Texts") of this same period. The Egyptians of this time refer to Jerusalem as an enemy to be cursed. Thus, the city must have been rather strong in Abraham's time to have called forth this expression of hatred. Jerusalem is also referred to in the Tel el-Amarna tablets and in numerous Assyrian and Babylonian documents.

Jerusalem, of course, is still occupied. Archaeological investigations of its buried layers thus have not been as extensive as they could have been otherwise. Nevertheless, some truly remarkable discoveries have been made. In 1880, a schoolboy accidentally discovered an inscription at the Siloam Tunnel, also called Hezekiah's Tunnel. This was a passage for water, which was cut through the rock of the mount under the ancient city. The tunnel led from the Gihon fountain on the east overlooking the Kedron Valley, to the southern end of Jerusalem. The inscription mentioned that the tunnel was "1,200 cubits" long. Since it measures about 1,750 feet, the cubit was equal to 17½ inches. Also, the inscription told how

SILOAM INSCRIPTION

the tunnel was dug—with workmen starting on both ends and meeting in the middle, much as modern tunnels are dug. It is one of the oldest Hebrew inscriptions known.

One of the most interesting discoveries pertaining to Jerusalem concerns its capture by David. This event is described in 2 Samuel 5:6–9:

The king and his men went to Jerusalem unto the Jebusites, the inhabitants of the land: which spake unto David, saying, Except thou take away the blind and the lame, thou shalt not come in hither: thinking, David cannot come in hither.

Nevertheless, David took the strong hold of Zion: the same is the city of David.

And David said on that day, Whosoever getteth up to the gutter, and smiteth the Jebusites, and the lame and the blind, that are hated of David's soul, he shall be chief and captain. Wherefore they said, The blind and the lame shall not come into the house.

So David dwelt in the fort, and called it the city of David. And David built round about from Millo and inward.

This passage has been interpreted in different ways. Most interpreters follow Josephus (see *Antiquities* VII.iii). He believed that the Jebusites were mocking David, implying that their defenses were so strong that feeble cripples and blind people were all that they would need to keep their city safe. On the other hand, a recent interpreter, Y. Yadin, has compared the practice of these Jebusites to certain oath-taking ceremonies of the Hittites. Hittite soldiers were made to swear allegiance to their king and queen in formal ceremonies. One ritual involved a priest's holding wax before a fire and saying: "Whoever breaks these oaths, let him melt like wax." Another one provided that soldiers who were disloyal were to become like blind men:

They parade in front of them [the soldiers] a blind woman and a deaf man and you [priests] speak as follows: 'See! here is a blind woman and a deaf man. Whoever does evil to the king and the queen, let the oaths seize him! Let them make him blind! Let them make him deaf! Let them blind him like a blind man! Let them deafen him like a deaf man! Let them annihilate him, the man himself together with his wife, his children, and his kin!'

Thus, Yadin suggests that the Jebusites by no means were overconfident that they could hold out against David. On the basis of these texts, he feels that the Jebusites were using magical formulas to curse David's forces to become blind and feeble so that David could not take their city.

The "gutter" or channel which David and his men followed to take the city has been identified as a vertical shaft which led down to the spring of Gihon, the main source of Jerusalem's water supply.

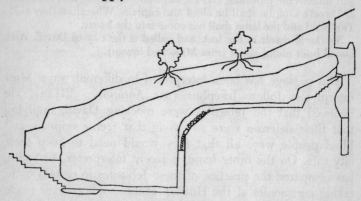

ROCK-CUT PASSAGE ABOVE VIRGIN'S FOUNT
("GIHON" OF THE OLD TESTAMENT)

People above the shaft could lower their vessels into the water safely, even during times of seige. The water collected along the bottom of the shaft and could be lifted into the safety of the city above. Apparently David's men made their way up the rough sides of the vertical shaft and thus conquered the city. This ingenious arrangement of the Jebusites was first discovered by the archaeological researches of Charles Warren.

Nineveh—Capital of the Assyrians

The capital of the Assyrians shifted at different periods from place to place, according to the whims of various monarchs. Some of the earlier capitals were Calah, Ashur, Dur-Sharrukin, and Nineveh. Nineveh was located on the east side of the Tigris River, at a spot which is today opposite the modern city of Mosul. The city fell in 612 B.C., and the site has not been inhabited since. Xenophon, the famous Greek historian, passed by the mound in 404 B.C. and spoke of the place as deserted. (It was then known as "Mespila." See *Anabasis* iii.4.10–12.)

With Nineveh's destruction, which was welcomed with great joy by the prophet Nahum, the Assyrian Empire began its complete disintegration: "Woe to the bloody city . . . there is a multitude of slain . . . there is none end of their corpses" (Nahum 3:1–3). The capital was briefly moved to Haran (where Abraham sojourned, see Gen. 11:31), which likewise fell in 608 B.C. Then finally, in desperation, the capital was moved to Carchemish, which fell in 605 B.C.

The new world power was Babylon. The new leader of the Babylonians, who defeated the combined forces of Assyria and Egypt at Carchemish in 605, was Nebuchadnezzar. Jeremiah noted Nebuchadnezzar's triumph at Carchemish (Jer. 46:1 ff.) and saw accurately that it was foolish for the Jews to resist accepting Nebuchadnezzar as the new ruler of the world.

Nineveh's remains consist of two great mounds, Kuyunjik and Nebi Yunus (the mound of the prophet Jonah). Early excavators at first mistakenly identified other places with Nineveh. During 1847–51, an English archaeologist, A. H. Layard, discovered the large palace of Sennacherib at Kuyunjik. He excavated seventy-one rooms of this palace, whose walls were lined with magnificent sculptured plaques depicting the victories of Sennacherib. Placed next to one another, the recovered plaques stretch in a straight line for approximately a mile and a half. They are deposited now in the British Museum.

Babylon—Capital of the Babylonians

Babylon was located on the Euphrates River about sixty miles south of the modern city of Baghdad. Like Nineveh, it was spread out over various mounds. It was north of the present-day village of Hilla, which, since around A.D. 1200, has been constructed with bricks from Babylon's ancient ruins. Two mounds, "Babil" and "al Qasr," represent some of the central parts of the ancient city. The name "Babel," which the ancient city was called, means "Gate of God." Josephus informs us that Babylon was inhabited as late as the New Testament period and that a small group of Jews still lived there (see *Antiquities* XVIII.ix.8).

Beginning in 1899, the German Oriental Society provided resources for large-scale excavations at Babylon which continued for eighteen years. The archaeologist in charge of this work was Robert Koldewey. Walter Andrae also carried on brilliant excavations at Babylon.

Babylon is referred to frequently in both the Old and New Testaments. The most famous king of Babylon, of course was Nebuchadnezzar II (605–562 B.C.). His palace, which was next to the Ishtar Gate, was excavated by the Germans. Countless tablets containing valuable ancient records were found there. Some of these mention the rations received by Jehoiachin and members of the royal family who were held captive there by Nebuchadnezzar.

Mesha (around 870–850 B.C.)

"And Mesha king of Moab was a sheepmaster, and rendered unto the king of Israel [Ahab] an hundred thousand lambs and an hundred thousand rams, with the wool. But it came to pass, when Ahab was dead, that the king of Moab rebelled against the king of Israel" (2 Kings 3:4–5).

In 1868, a large inscription was found at Dhiban, Mesha's capital city. In this monument, Mesha described how he was oppressed by Omri for many years but threw off Israel's burdensome yoke just before Ahab died. "Omri" was a dynastic name for the kings of Israel; thus, it was later applied to Jehu. Mesha's record of Israelite oppression matches the biblical account closely. Mesha also told how he destroyed the Jewish city of Ataroth and put all of its citizens to death, just as Joshua put the Canaanites to death. (See Josh. 6:21.)

Mesha said: "I am Mesha . . . King of Moab . . . as for Omri, King of Israel, he humbled Moab for many years, for Chemosh [the god of the Moabites] was angry at his land. And his son followed him and he also said 'I will humble Moab.' In my time he spoke thus, but I have triumphed over him and over his house." (See Pritchard, *Ancient Near Eastern Texts*, pp. 320 f.)

Sargon (722–705 B.C.)

"In the year that Tartan [the commander-in-chief of the Assyrian army] came unto Ashdod, (when Sargon the King of Assyria sent him,) and fought against Ashdod and took it" (Isa. 20:1).

Mention has been made of Botta's recovery of Sargon's palace north of Nineveh. Besides Ashdod's capture, Sargon also boasted of taking Samaria in 722–721 B.C.: "At the beginning of my royal reign . . . the town of the Samaritans I conquered . . . I led away as prisoners 27,290 of its citizens

. . . this town I rebuilt better than it was before and placed therein people from [other] countries which I had conquered. I placed an officer of mine as governor over them and imposed upon them tribute" (see Pritchard, *Ancient Near Eastern Texts,* pp. 284 f.).

It is even possible that Sargon's brother, Shalmaneser V, who preceded him on the throne of Assyria (727–722 B.C.), actually took the city of Samaria. Since Shalmaneser died about this time, Sargon could boast that he himself took Samaria with no fear of protest from his dead brother!

Sennacherib (705–681 B.C.)

"Now in the fourteenth year of king Hezekiah [701 B.C.] did Sennacherib king of Assyria come up against all the fenced cities of Judah, and took them. . . . And Hezekiah gave him all the silver that was found in the house of the Lord, and . . . cut off the gold from the doors of the temple of the Lord, and from the pillars . . . and gave it to the king of Assyria" (2 Kings 18:13–16).

Sennacherib also gives us an account of his capture of Jerusalem and of his imposition of tribute upon Hezekiah:

As to Hezekiah the Jew, he did not submit to my yoke, I laid siege to 46 of his strong cities . . . and to countless small villages. . . . I drove out of them 200,150 people. . . . Hezekiah himself I made a prisoner in Jerusalem, his royal residence, like a bird in a cage . . . I increased the tribute and the presents due to me as his overlord . . . Hezekiah . . . did send me, later, to Nineveh, my lordly city, together with 30 talents of gold, 800 talents of silver, precious stones . . . couches inlaid with ivory . . . and all kinds of valuable treasures (see Pritchard, *Ancient Near Eastern Texts,* p. 288).

The records of Sennacherib are meager toward the end of his reign. The Bible indicates that he made a later invasion into Palestine, at which time he was defeated. He would not want to boast about this event under any circumstance, but it is referred to in Isaiah 37:36. The death angel took the lives of 185,000 of his soldiers. It seems that this refers to a period after 689 B.C., since Tirhakah (cf. Isa. 37:9), who came out to give aid to the Jews, did not become king of Egypt until 689 B.C.

Nebuchadnezzar (605–561 B.C.)

"The word of the Lord which came to Jeremiah . . . against Egypt, against the army of Pharaoh-necho king of Egypt, which was by the river Euphrates in Carchemish, which Nebuchadrezzar king of Babylon smote in the fourth year of Jehoiakim the son of Josiah king of Judah" (Jer. 46:1–2).

Mention has already been made of the fact that Carchemish was the last capital of the Assyrians. Nebuchadnezzar destroyed the combined armies of Assyria and Egypt in 605 B.C., and Babylon became the new world ruler. It is easy to understand why Necho, king of Egypt, would want Assyria to survive. He wanted to help bolster Assyria so that he could use her against Babylon. If Assyria could serve as a buffer against Babylon, Egypt, not Babylon, would rule the world! Nebuchadnezzar's records tell us how he defeated the Assyrians and Egyptians at Carchemish:

Nebuchadnezzar the crown prince mustered the Babylonian army and took command of the troops; he marched to Carchemish which is on the banks of the Euphrates, and crossed the river to go against the Egyptian army which lay in Carchemish . . . he accomplished their defeat . . . the rest of the Egyptian army . . . escaped. . . . In the district of Hamath the Babylonian troops overtook and defeated them (see Wiseman, *Chronicles of Chaldean Kings in the British Musuem,* pp. 67–69).

Second Kings 24:1 informs us that Jehoiakim rebelled against Nebuchadnezzar (around 601 B.C.). Nebuchadnezzar had lost a battle that year to the Egyptians, but he reorganized his forces and came back into Judea. He besieged and captured Jerusalem in 597 B.C. "Nebuchadnezzar king of Babylon came against the city [of Jerusalem], and . . . did besiege it . . . and the king of Babylon took him [Jehoiachin, the king of Judah] in the eighth year of his [Nebuchadnezzar's reign" (2 Kings 24:11–12). Newly translated sections of the Babylonian Chronicle tell us the very day and year when this took place:

In the seventh year [598 B.C.], the month of Kislimu, the King of Akkad [Nebuchadnezzar] mustered his troops, marched to Hatti-land [Palestine] and encamped against the city of Judah [Jerusalem] and on the second day of the month of Addaru he seized the city and captured the king [Jehoiachin]. He appointed there a king of his own choice [Zedekiah], received its heavy tribute and sent them to Babylon (see Wiseman, *Chronicles of Chaldean Kings in the British Museum,* p. 73).

Jehoiachin (598–550 B.C.)

Clay tablets have been discovered in Babylon which tell of the amount of rations Jehoiachin received from the royal allotments of food. Even though Jehoiachin was in captivity, he was regarded as the true king of the Jews and is called "Yaukin, king of the land of Judah" on these tablets. Five of his sons are mentioned.

7

The Text of the New Testament

Archaeological work has many facets; for example, it includes the study of ancient biblical manuscripts. Numerous biblical manuscripts have been discovered.

Tischendorf and the Codex Sinaiticus

Constantine Tischendorf was born in Germany in 1815 and died there in 1874. His greatest contribution consisted in discovering and editing ancient biblical manuscripts. He was educated and licensed to lecture at the University of Leipzig, where he concentrated on Greek studies. In 1844, he made a journey to the Holy Land in search of ancient biblical manuscripts.

Tischendorf's name will be forever linked with the famous Sinaiticus Bible, his greatest discovery. He first discovered parts of this manuscript in 1844, while visiting the library of St. Catherine's Monastery at Mount Sinai. He described his remarkable discovery as follows:

I perceived in the middle of the great hall a large and wide basket full of old parchments; and the librarian, who was a man of information, told me that two heaps of papers like these, mouldered by time, had already been committed to the flames. What was my surprise to find amid this heap of papers a considerable number of sheets of a copy of the Old Testament in Greek, which seemed to me to be one of the most ancient that I had ever seen. The authorities of the convent allowed me to possess myself of a third of these parchments, or about forty-three sheets, all the more readily as they were destined for the fire. But I could not get them to yield up possession of the remainder. The too lively satisfaction which I had displayed had aroused their suspicions.

On his return to Europe, Tischendorf could not forget this manuscript. He published the leaves which he had been permitted to keep but discreetly said nothing about where he had secured them. He went back to Sinai in 1853. This time the custodians of the library cautiously kept their precious manuscript from him.

Tischendorf returned to Sinai for the third time in 1859. He brought on this trip a recommendation from the Czar of Russia, head of the Orthodox Church, with which the monastery was connected. On the last night of his visit, the librarian permitted him to see the leaves which he had seen fifteen years before, but which now had been restored to the whole manuscript from which they had been detached. The manuscript contained the books of the Bible, plus the books of Barnabas and Hermas. Concealing his great excitement, he asked permission to take the manuscript to his room to look at it "in his leisure." He then stayed up the whole night copying from it!

He notes: "There by myself I could give way to the transport of joy which I felt. I knew that I held in my hand the most precious biblical treasure in existence—a document whose age and importance exceeded that of all the manuscripts which I had ever examined during twenty years' study of the subject." He was at length able to persuade the monks of the Sinai monastery to send the manuscript to the Czar of Russia as a gift. In turn, the Czar gave large sums to the monastery and commissioned Tischendorf to edit and to issue a facsimile copy of the manuscript.

Under what circumstances this precious manuscript was acquired by the Sinai monastery it is impossible to say. The character of the script and other evidences indicate that it was first produced around A.D. 350, by various scribes and correctors. It was probably made at either Alexandria in Egypt or Caesarea in Palestine.

The Sinaiticus Bible was sold by Russia to the British Museum in 1933 for £100,000. It is one of the prize trophies of the Museum. It is kept in a glass-covered case with a velvet cover. The cover is designed so that maximum light can be excluded, lest it cause even slight fading.

The Discovery of Papyri: Grenfell and Hunt

The modern word "paper" is derived from "papyrus." The ancient Egyptians made their paper from papyrus, which was a reed plant that grew along the banks of the Nile. The outer bark of the plant could be peeled off, like sugar cane, and then the inner core, or pith, would be sliced lengthwise into thin strips. A layer of strips would be placed side by side. Another layer was made by placing strips at a right angle. There was enough gum in the plant to make the strips adhere when they were pressed together. When the strips dried, they were trimmed evenly to form a sheet for writing. The finished pages would be glued together to form continuous scrolls.

Papyrus was used as a writing material by the Egyptians at least as early as 3000 B.C. Since Egypt has a dry climate, vast quantities of papyrus in tombs or even covered by the sand have been marvelously preserved. About the beginning of the Christian period, books were made which resemble our modern "leaf books." This form of a book is called a codex. Copyists of the New Testament used the codex form before the end of the first century, perhaps indicating that some of the New Testament authors originally used it.

The serious recovery of the Egyptian papyri treasures started around the end of the last century. In 1895–96, B. P. Grenfell and A. S. Hunt dug for papyri in the rubbish heaps of modern Behnesa, in the Faiyum district of Egypt, about one hundred miles southwest of Cairo. This town was called Oxyrhynchus in the Greco-Roman period and was an early center of Christianity. Sensational results were obtained there. In following years, this same team excavated other Egyptian sites, such as Tebtunis and el-Hibeh. Literally tons of ancient papyri were recovered in these digs. The collection is so vast that its publication has not yet been completed. Many of the fragments are biblical in nature. Most papyrus writings, of course, are letters, business records, tax lists, receipts, or deal with other daily matters.

Even those materials which deal with daily affairs are of great value. Census lists, for example, help us to know that it was the Roman practice to have a census taken every fourteen years. Historical data such as this, when applied to the gospel account, suggest the likely time of Jesus' birth as about 8–7 B.C., since census documents from A.D. 20, 34, and others are known.

The vocabulary of the New Testament can be better understood in light of papyrus records. We get this better grasp by seeing how biblical words were used by other writers of the Roman period. One of the most thorough investigators of this branch of biblical study was Adolf Deissmann.

In recent years, many papyrus materials, some of which give us our earliest portions of the Bible, have come to light.

A Fragment of John's Gospel (P 52)

The oldest portion of the New Testament which has been discovered thus far comes from the Gospel of John. In 1920, B. P. Grenfell acquired a small papyrus fragment which measured only 2½ by 3½ inches. The nature of this fragment lay unrecognized until 1935. C. H. Roberts, a reader of Greek manuscripts, came across it while examining the papyrus materials possessed by the John Rylands Library in Manchester, England.

In studying the fragment, Roberts was able to detect that it was very early, and that it contained a few verses from the Gospel of John (18:31–34,37,38). Other authorities agreed with the early date assigned to it; the fragment was written between A.D. 110–50. As far as can be determined, this fragment shows that the text of John's Gospel was practically the same then as our present critical Greek text of the New Testament.

Fragments of an Unknown Gospel (Egerton Papyrus 2)

Also in 1935, another remarkable discovery came to light. The British Museum had acquired in the previous year four strange fragments of papyri which dealt with events in the life of Jesus, some of which were not recorded in the present four Gospels. Yet, at the same time, this *Unknown Gospel* included several incidents and quotations of Jesus' life which were previously known in the New Testament Gospels. The work thus seems to have been an early attempt to make a composite gospel from numerous materials then at hand.

The *Unknown Gospel* also dates between A.D. 125–50. Some critics had denied that John's Gospel, in particular, was written as early as the first century. Since various quotations from John appear in this *Unknown Gospel,* and in light of the Rylands fragment, the theory of a date later than A.D. 100 for John's Gospel has become totally unacceptable!

The Chester Beatty Papyri (P 45; P 46; P 47)

In 1930, a collection of biblical manuscripts from an ancient church library was discovered in Egypt, none of which is dated later than the fourth century. Chester Beatty, an Australian who lived in London, acquired a large number of these manuscripts, which are today in the Beatty Library in Dublin, Ireland. Manuscripts in this collection include the Old Testament books of Genesis, Numbers, Deuteronomy, Esther, Isaiah, Jeremiah, Ezekiel, Daniel, and Ecclesiastes. The New Testament portions include large sections of the Gospels, the book of Acts (P [45]), Paul's letters (P [46]), and Revelation (P [47]).

The copy of Paul's letters in the Beatty materials dates to about A.D. 200. The value of the Chester Beatty materials can be realized when it is recalled, for example, that our next biblical manuscript source for Paul's letters dates to the beginning of the fourth century A.D. Thus, these documents reduce in half the time lapse between Codex Vaticanus (an early Bible dating around A.D. 325, slightly before Codex Sinaiticus) and this apostle (around A.D. 50). Again, there are a few variants between the Beatty manuscripts and other biblical manuscripts, but none of these affects any major biblical teaching. They consist mostly in errors of spellings, rearrangements, omissions, and so on. For example, the doxology of Romans 16:25–27 is placed at the end of chapter 15 in the Beatty manuscript of Paul's letters (P [46]).

The Bodmer Papyri (P [66]; P [74]; P [75])

It is no exaggeration to say that what the Dead Sea Scrolls have been for the early text of the Old Testament, the Chester Beatty and Bodmer materials have been for the early text of the New Testament. Like the Beatty manuscripts, the Bodmer scripts were found in Egypt, and in many respects are similar. Both collections include materials from the Old and New Testaments, and they date roughly to the same time.

Two copies of John's Gospel are included in the Bodmer

manuscripts (P 66 and P 75). Both copies date around A.D. 175–225. One is a separate book and is more complete (P 66); the other (P 75) is joined with the Gospel of Luke (P 74) to form a single book.

The more complete copy of John (P 66) was published in 1956. It agrees substantially with the present Greek Bible, which has been transmitted through the centuries. Both P 66 and P 75 omit the passages about the angel's stirring the water (John 5:3–4) and the woman taken in adultery (7:53 to 8:11), but so do all other reliable manuscripts.

The shorter copy of John (P 75) has an interesting reading: "Jesus therefore said again, Verily, verily I say to you, I am the *shepherd* [not 'door'] of the sheep." (John 10:7).

The Bodmer copy of the Gospel of Luke (P 74) is well preserved. It contains Luke 3:18 to 18:18 and 22:4 to the end of the Gospel. The text of Luke, like that of John, is essentially that of later Greek manuscripts. All of these manuscripts show how faithfully the Bible was transmitted by later copyists.

Minor variants are found: Jesus sent out 72 disciples (not 70) in Luke 10:1,17; in the "Parable of Lazarus and the Rich Man," the rich man's name is "Neues" (Luke 16:19). The description of Jesus in Gethsemane says nothing about the strengthening angel nor "the bloody sweat" (Luke 22:43–44), but this section is omitted by many other reliable Greek manuscripts also.

8

The Dead Sea Scrolls

▲▲▲

In the summer of 1947, while searching for a stray goat, Muhammad adh-Dhib, an Arab shepherd, noticed a small opening in a rock cliffside near the Dead Sea. Out of curiosity, he threw a rock through the opening, and hearing a loud, shattering noise, rushed off in fear. He soon returned with a companion, and together they crawled through the opening which led into a cave. Scattered about were several jars— some standing upright with scrolls inside, some resting on their sides, and others shattered. Pieces of leather containing writings and broken pottery were also found.

Gathering several scrolls, these shepherds left the cave. They showed their discoveries to various friends and finally sold them for less than ten dollars to a Bethlehem cobbler named Kando. Not knowing the value or nature of these documents, Kando sent a scrap of one of the scrolls to a fellow dealer in antiquities at Jerusalem. Late in November, 1947, this man showed the scrap to a Jewish archaeologist, E. L. Sukenik, who was connected with the Hebrew University at Jerusalem.

In the 1920s, Sukenik had attended the American School of Oriental Research and had studied with W. F. Albright, a foremost authority on old Semitic writing. Sukenik had mastered the Jewish alphabet as it was written in the time of

Jesus. Having studied carefully the writings on Jewish tombs and coffins which were known to have been constructed in Jesus' time, Sukenik knew at a glance the value of the scrap.

As a Jew, Sukenik knew he would be taking his life in his hands to visit Bethlehem, an Arab community. Hostilities which finally led to the Arab-Israeli war in 1947–48 were intensifying. But in spite of the danger, he went and saw the scrolls which the dealer had in his possession. He purchased three of them and two complete jars in which they had been contained. These included a partial copy of Isaiah; a "war" scroll, dealing with a future war to take place between God's elect and surrounding enemy nations; and a group of thanksgiving psalms, somewhat similar to the Old Testament book of Psalms but much later.

Sukenik wrote in his diary of December 1, 1947: "I have read a little more on the leathers. I tremble as I think about them. This may be one of the greatest discoveries in the country: a discovery of which we could never have dreamt."

Four other scrolls were sold by Kando to his spiritual leader, Archbishop Samuel, in Jerusalem. These included a complete copy of Isaiah; a *Manual of Discipline*, a list of regulations for the religious group which wrote the scrolls; a *Commentary of Habakkuk*; and an *Apocryphon of Genesis*, containing legendary material on the patriarchs. Sukenik had opportunity to see these materials but was not financially able to purchase them.

Archbishop Samuel took his scrolls to the American School of Oriental Reasearch in Jerusalem. Two students there, William Brownlee and John Trever, were permitted to look at them and to take photographs. These photographs were sent to W. F. Albright at Johns Hopkins University. He pronounced the scrolls authentic and the "greatest manuscript discovery of all time."

At length, Samuel brought his scrolls to America, hoping to

sell them. Various institutions, such as Yale University, were approached. Fearing possible legal complications, they refused to buy them. After all, the scrolls had been taken out of Jordan in violation of a national law, and the government might file suit. No antiquities law, however, could be enforced against Israel, which is in a state of war with Jordan. Thus, the scrolls still possessed by Archbishop Samuel were eventually purchased by Sukenik's son, Y. Yadin. They are now on display at the Hebrew University at Jerusalem, Israel.

Since the recovery of the first scrolls from the cave (now called Cave I) by the wandering Arab shepherds, ten other caves have been explored in this vicinity. They have yielded thousands of fragments of ancient manuscripts, plus other, more complete scrolls. These caves are located near an abandoned heap of ruins known today as Khirbet Qumran, nine miles due south of Jericho. An archaeological team, led by Lanchester Harding and Père Roland de Vaux, excavated this site between 1952 and 1956.

The scrolls have a definite relationship to the site which was excavated. Most of them were no doubt produced at Qumran, since writing tables, ink wells, and so on, were found there. The question arises: "What kind of people lived at Qumram and produced these scrolls?"

Most of the Qumran scrolls are biblical or reveal a peculiar religious character. As a matter of fact, every book of the Old Testament except Esther is among them. Therefore, the inhabitants of this site must have been a religious sect.

There is reason to believe that Qumran was a center for the Essenes, a religious group which flourished during the time of Christ. They are mentioned by Josephus, Philo, and Pliny, who lived and wrote in this era. These writers affirm that the Essenes lived in this vicinity of the Dead Sea. Besides, the Dead Sea Scrolls provide various documents which seem to have originated with the Essenes. They tell what the

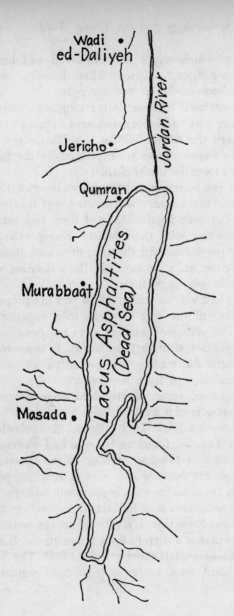

Wadi ed-Daliyeh •

Jericho •

Qumran •

Jordan River

Lacus Asphaltites (Dead Sea)

Murabba'at •

Masada •

**FIND SPOTS
OF ANCIENT
MANUSCRIPTS
AROUND THE
DEAD SEA**

religious group which wrote them believed and how they carried on their religious practices. These beliefs closely parallel what we know to be Essene concepts.

The New Testament mentions other religious groups, such as the Pharisees and Sadducees, but says nothing about the Essenes. Perhaps the silence of the New Testament writers concerning the Essenes is to be explained by the fact that they lived apart from the world of their day.

The Essenes can be compared to modern ascetics. Even the spot where their main center was located was relatively isolated and off the main roads. Many of them did not marry. They were secretive with their beliefs. Rising early in the morning, they prayed toward the sun; they took their meals together in a community dining hall. Each member was assigned a specific job to perform.

The Essenes had various ranks, and it was not proper for a younger member of the sect to speak to a superior unless called upon. The younger members were not even supposed to come into contact with their superiors. Essenes refrained from taking oaths. No trading was permitted with outsiders except by permission of their supervisors.

The Essenes were especially rigid in their allegiance to Moses. They considered it a crime deserving of death to speak against Moses or his laws. They rejected the priesthood of the Jerusalem Temple, for some priests had married their nieces in violation of the law of Moses. The Essenes were much more legalistic than the Pharisees in their interpretation of the sabbath commandment. They carried sabbath observance so far as to believe that it violated the law for them to relieve their bowels on this day! The Pharisees were reasonable enough to permit a man to lift a fallen animal from a pit on the sabbath (see Matt. 12:11; Luke 14:5). The Essenes, on the other hand, went so far in their rigid regulations to declare it to be a sin even to lift a man from a pit on the sabbath.

Some modern interpreters have emphasized similarities between John the Baptist and Jesus and the Essenes. There are, however, more differences than similarities. For example, if Jesus criticized the Pharisees for their unbending legalism, his denunciations of the Essenes would necessarily have been much more severe.

While the reader of the New Testament may gain much by examining the writings of the Essenes, these documents do not present any personality which can compare favorably with Jesus. Rather, the Dead Sea Scrolls show us how vastly superior Jesus' view of salvation is from that of the Essenes.

The Essenes were instructed to "hate" every person who was not a member of their sect. The hierarchy which they observed was likewise totally foreign to the Christian pattern. Essene "baptisms" were practiced daily, unlike the once-for-all pattern of the Christian ordinance. The Essenes looked to the future to be saved; the Christians looked back to the redemptive work of God in Christ, as well as to the future. These are only a few of the differences that sharply distinguish Essene practices from those of the early Christians.

The Dead Sea Scrolls supply us with the most ancient copies of the Old Testament that we have. Until the Scrolls were discovered, the oldest and most complete Hebrew copies of the Bible dated as late as the ninth century A.D. Formerly, therefore, the most ancient copies of the Old Testament were not in Hebrew but in Greek.

Some of the Hebrew Scriptures were translated into Greek shortly after the time of Alexander the Great. Alexander had encouraged large numbers of Jews to settle in his Egyptian capital city of Alexandria. These Egyptian Jews soon gave up speaking Hebrew and readily adopted the Greek language. Accordingly, the Septuagint, the Greek version of the Old Testament, was very popular among Egyptian Jews. The Dead Sea Scrolls have shown that the Septuagint is an extremely important witness to the Old Testament text. Ancient Hebrew manuscripts, which support the Septuagint version consistently, have been discovered at Qumran.

It should be realized that it was primarily the Greek Septuagint that was quoted by New Testament authors. H. B. Swete, in his *Introduction to the Old Testament in Greek*, estimates that there are 160 such quotations in the New Testament.

Some New Testament quotations from the Old Testament are puzzling. For example, Stephen quotes the Old Testament to the effect that "75" people went with Jacob into Egypt from Palestine (cf. Acts 7:14). The Hebrew text, which has been followed in our English translations, states that "70" people went with him (cf. Ex. 1:5). The Dead Sea Scrolls now help to explain this difference in numbers. Old Hebrew manuscripts, dating two hundred years before Jesus' time, recently found at Qumran, likewise read "75," just as the Septuagint had it. Thus, Stephen was not in error (nor Luke, the author of Acts), as some have supposed.

In Hebrews 1:6, we read that the Scriptures say: "Let all the angels of God worship him." This statement cannot be found in modern Hebrew Bibles. Yet, it was found in copies of the Hebrew Old Testament in the time of Jesus, for the Dead Sea Scrolls place this verse after Deuteronomy 32:43! The Septuagint had preserved these words in this place also.

So the Dead Sea Scrolls have shown that the Septuagint must be taken seriously as a reliable witness to the Old Testament text. Not all of the manuscripts at Qumran were in Hebrew, for a few Greek fragments of the Septuagint have also been found there.

The Scrolls do not destroy our confidence in the general reliability of the transmission of the Old Testament. This might seem strange in a day when only that which is sensational tends to draw attention. Automobiles, soap powder, toothpaste, electrical appliances, and so on, must be radically different from "last year's type" to have appeal!

The Scrolls have demonstrated that the Old Testament used by Jesus and his disciples is essentially the same Old Testament which we have today. There were, and still are of course, certain variants between the Greek Septuagint and the familiar Hebrew text. But these do not affect any major doctrine of the Old or New Testament. Nor does there need to be any doubt concerning the message and challenge of the Old Testament as applied to our own lives.

The Dead Sea Scrolls help to solve certain problems which relate to the *dating* of the Old Testament books.

For example, many writers suggest that the book of Ecclesiastes was composed around 200 to 180 B.C. or even later. Graetz believed that the author of Ecclesiastes lived in the time of Hillel, shortly before Jesus. Certain fragments of this book have been found at Qumran (in Cave IV) which must date around 150 B.C.! All theories of authorship for Ecclesiastes, therefore, must now be tested by this new discovery.

Some writers likewise have dated many of the psalms in the late Hellenistic or Maccabean period (around 200–63 B.C.). One Qumran manuscript, which was copied from older sources about this very period, shows basically the same contents for the psalms which we have in our present Bibles. Thus, the contents of psalms had already been established by Maccabean times. However, it should be said that the book of Psalms was not always arranged *in the same order* as our present Bible has it. One extra psalm (151) was included in the Greek Septuagint, and this psalm also appears in Hebrew in a manuscript from Cave XI.

In summary, the Dead Sea Scrolls enable us to understand the religious beliefs and historical background of Palestine in the first century. They supply important geographical information and give abundant comparative materials for studying Hebrew and Aramaic languages as used in Jesus' day. Many scrolls are still unpublished, and many are still being discovered. To appreciate fully their value, intensive research must continue.

9

Inscriptions and Coins

▲▲▲

A recent comment by W. F. Albright on the value of inscriptions deserves attention: "Nothing can eliminate the stubborn fact that the Bible is a written document and will thus be illuminated most directly by written sources, especially when they belong to the same period."

Some notice has already been given to certain inscriptions which add to our understanding of the Old Testament. The New Testament message also takes on new color and vitality in the light of hundreds of inscriptions which are related to its background. Some inscriptions of great importance have been found in recent years.

The Pilate Inscription

Almost by accident, Italian archaeologists working in the theater at Caesarea discovered an inscription mentioning Pontius Pilate. Antonio Frova, the director, had asked his workers to wash down part of the excavation with a hose. In the process, the inscription came to light. Only four lines could be restored: "The Tiberieum of the Caesareans Pontius Pilate Praefect of Judea has given." No other inscription is known which mentions Pilate. Of course, Pilate is referred to by contemporary first-century historians, such as Josephus, Philo, and Tacitus.

This inscription is important for two special reasons. It informs us that Pilate was a "prefect," at least in the early part of his career. Josephus calls Pilate a "procurator." There was, of course, very little difference in the duties connected with these offices. "Prefect" was the more common term in the time of Augustus but gradually gave way to the title of "procurator" by the time of the Emperor Claudius. The New Testament writers consistently refer to Pilate as "governor." This was a more neutral term which could be used interchangeably to refer to either "prefect" or "procurator." Probably Pilate's title in office changed from that of "prefect" to "procurator" and this is the reason the New Testament writers chose to use the term "governor."

More important is the mention the Pilate Inscription gives of the "Tiberieum," which Pilate built in honor of Tiberius. This refers to a temple which perhaps would be used for purposes of emperor worship. We are enabled by this new information to better understand Pilate's role in the crucifixion of Jesus.

Josephus informs us that Pilate had frequent trouble with his subjects, and for this the Jews complained to Tiberius. Pilate was naturally anxious to show himself loyal to Tiberius. This temple likely required several years to construct and was probably in process during Jesus' earthly ministry. The Jews used Pilate's "patriotism" as their main lever when they pushed him to sentence Jesus to death, "If thou let this man go, thou art not Caesar's friend" (John 19:12).

Lysanias

An inscription discovered on the site of Abila, which was the capital of the district of Abilene, settled an argument.

Luke 3:1 informs us that a certain Lysanias ruled various areas in Syria and Palestine at the time John the Baptist began his preaching ministry. Josephus mentions that a king by the name of "Lysanias," who ruled over the same general area, had been put to death around 36 B.C. by Mark Anthony (who suspected Lysanias of being in a conspiracy with the Parthians). Critics found a problem here—a contradiction between Luke and Josephus. Many believed Josephus to be right and Luke wrong.

We now know that both Luke and Josephus were right. The inscription mentioned a later Lysanias who lived during the time of Tiberius and his mother Livia: "In behalf of the welfare of the Augustan Rulers [Tiberius and Livia] and all of their household, Nymphaios, a freedman of Lysanias the Tetrarch, has built the street . . . and erected the temple."

Livia, Tiberius' mother, died in A.D. 29; therefore, the inscription can be dated no later than this time. On the other hand, Augustus died in A.D. 14; after this time Livia became associated with Tiberius, the new emperor. Together they were called the "Augustan Rulers," just as the inscription reads. It was in this period, then, that "Lysanias the Tetrarch" reigned—sometime between A.D. 14–29.

Luke and this inscription both designate this Lysanias as a tetrarch. The earlier Lysanias was called "king" and did not rule over Abilene. Thus, Luke's statements seem to be absolutely correct in light of this information and on the basis of other known inscriptions.

Gallio

The apostle Paul frequently came into contact with famous Roman personalities. One of these personalities was Gallio (cf. Acts 18:12).

Immediately after Gallio arrived in Corinth, the Roman capital of Greece, the Jews brought a lawsuit against Paul. They accused him of starting a new religion, which was illegal, according to the law of the Romans. Gallio refused to hear their case and threw it out of court (cf. v. 16).

Gallio was an older brother of Seneca, the famous philosopher who later became one of Nero's advisers. Seneca dedicated two books to Gallio (*On Anger* and *The Happy Life*). Gallio is also mentioned by Roman historians Pliny, Tacitus, and Dio Cassius.

Around A.D. 1900, a mutilated inscription was found at Delphi. It begins:

Tiberius Claudius Caesar Augustus Germanicus, High Priest, holding the power of tribune for the 12th time, acclaimed Emperor the 26th time, father of the country, consul for the 5th time, censor, salutes the city of Delphi. For a long while I have been enthusiastic for the city of Delphi . . . and well disposed to it from the beginning [of my reign] and I have continuously observed the worship of the Pythian Apollo . . . but such things as are now talked about, even those bickerings of the citizens . . . just as Lucius Junius Gallio, my friend and proconsul of Achaia has written. . . .

Mention of Gallio as being proconsul during the time of the twenty-sixth acclamation of Claudius as Emperor is most important. This dates the year in which Gallio was in Corinth as January-July of A.D. 52, thus determining a definite date in Paul's life.

The Warning Inscription from Herod's Temple

In Acts 21:26–30, we read of Paul's visit to the Temple in Jerusalem. Certain Jewish enemies falsely accused Paul of taking a Gentile into the Temple, thus defiling it (v. 28). A mob gathered and tried to kill Paul (v. 31). Even though Paul quickly was taken in hand by Roman soldiers who guarded the Temple (v. 32), the mob cried out for Paul to be killed (v. 36).

Josephus, in describing Herod's Temple, informs us that inscriptions were placed at the exits of the Court of the Gentiles which led to the Temple:

When you go through these [first] cloisters, unto the second [court of the] temple, there was a partition made of stone all round, whose height was three cubits: its construction was very elegant; upon it stood pillars, at equal distances from one another, declaring the law of purity, some in Greek, and some in Roman letters, that "no foreigner should go within that sanctuary;" for that second [court of the] temple was called "the Sanctuary," and was ascended to by fourteen steps from the first court. (*War* V.v.2; see also, *Against Apion* ii.8)

In 1871, the French archaeologist C. Clermont-Ganneau found a complete Greek copy of one of these inscriptions and in 1935 another fragmentary one was discovered.

The inscription reads: "No Gentile is permitted to enter within the protective wall and enclosure which surrounds the Temple. But, whoever is caught doing so shall himself be responsible for his death which shall follow (immediately)."

The inscription is self-explanatory. We notice in another passage of Josephus that even if a man were a Roman citizen (which Paul was) he had no appeal from this sentence of death (see *War* VI.ii.4). Thus, this inscription helps modern readers to understand perfectly the circumstances of Paul's arrest, imprisonment, and the charge against him at his trial.

Sergius Paullus (or "Paulus")

On Paul's first missionary journey (about A.D. 45), he came into contact with Sergius Paulus, the Roman proconsul (governor) of Cyprus, whose headquarters were at Paphos (cf. Acts 13:6–12). Many inscriptions have been found which various interpreters have referred to this particular "Sergius Paulus."

One of the early ambassadors from the United States to Cyprus was L. Palma de Cesnola. He was also an ardent collector of antiquities and found at Soli on Cyprus a poorly preserved inscription which can be read only with great difficulty:

Apollonius to his father . . ., and to his mother, Aristocleia.
Apollonius has made the enclosure and the family vault according
to their instructions for himself and for his sons. He has served as
high priest of the city of Soli, as chief of police, as town clerk, as
collector of taxes, and as keeper of the town archives. Erected in
the year 13, on the 25th of Demarchexousios [the 8th month in the
calendar of Cyprus]. Having served as censor, he set in order the
senate in the 10th year of the proconsul Paulus.

Many able scholars have seen this as a genuine reference
to Sergius Paulus. If so, the inscription would probably date
around A.D. 50–55, since Paul came in contact with him around
A.D. 45, perhaps after Paulus already had been in office a few
years. It is probably best to recognize that the Paulus of this
inscription may not be the one mentioned in Acts.

One inscription has been found, however, which mentions
a certain "L. Sergius Paullus" as one of the curators of the
Tiber River during the time of Claudius. There is much
greater likelihood that this inscription refers to the official
whom Paul met. The date of this inscription fits what we
know of Sergius Paulus in the book of Acts. The governors
appointed for the provinces usually came from Rome. Nothing
decisive can be determined by the differences in the way
the name was spelled ("Paulus" or "Paullus"), since minor
variations of this type were common at this time.

Quirinius

One of the most interesting statements in the New Testament concerns Quirinius. Luke mentions that Jesus was born
while "Cyrenius was governor of Syria" (2:2). Josephus mentions that Quirinius became governor of Syria around A.D. 6.
But this seems to be too late a time for the governorship that
Luke had in mind.

Throughout Luke's writings famous men are mentioned
and Quirinius is a good case in point. Various Roman historians

likewise have much to say about Quirinius. For example, Tacitus (*Annals* III.48) gives us very valuable information about his funeral, which was paid for by public expense in A.D. 21:

> Around this time Tiberius wrote to the senate, making request that a public funeral might be decreed to Sulpicius Quirinius. . . . He was born at Lanuvium, a municipal town: he distinguished himself by his military services, had considerable talents for business, and was raised by Augustus to the honor of the consulship. Having afterwards stormed and taken the strongholds of the Homanadeis in Cilicia, he obtained triumphal honors. He attended Gaius Caesar in his expedition to Armenia. . . . But the character of Quirinius was held in no esteem . . . and the sordid avarice of the man, even in old age, and in the height of his power, left a stain upon his memory.

Many inscriptions have been found in Asia Minor (modern Turkey) which definitely show that Quirinius was in Cilicia and surrounding regions, just as Tacitus reported. Moreover, at this time, Cilicia and Syria were not only adjoining but related provinces! On the basis of inscriptions, it is known that Quirinius was in the area around 10–8 B.C.

Inscriptions also show that Quirinius took a census in Apamea in Syria (it is not certain whether this is the census of A.D. 6 or an earlier census around 8-7 B.C.): "On command of Quirinius I have carried out the census in Apamea, a city-state of one hundred and seventeen thousand citizens. Likewise I was sent by Quirinius to march against the Itureans, and conquered their citadel on Lebanon mountain."

Some writers have objected to Luke's statement that Quirinius took a census in Judea, since it was under Herod at this time. But Apamea, like Judea, was also autonomous (self-governing), as its coins indicate; yet, it was forced to submit to the dreaded census as shown by the inscription. Moreover, after 8 B.C., Herod the Great lost his standing with

Augustus and was treated as a subject-king, according to Josephus.

A famous inscription is also known, called the *Lapis Tiburtinus*, which many able historians have interpreted as referring to Quirinius. This inscription was found in Rome in 1828, and is here translated:

[?P. Sulpicius Quirinius?] consul . . .; as proconsul obtained Crete and Cyrene as a province . . .; as legate of the divine Augustus, obtaining Syria and Phoenicia he waged war with the tribe of Homonadeis who had killed Amyntas the k[ing; when he returned into the domin]ion of the Emperor Caesar Augustus and the Roman people, the senate [decreed] thanksgivings [to the immortal gods] on account of the two success[ful accomplishments] and triumphal ornaments to him; as proconsul he ob[tained] Asia as a province; as the legate of the divine Augustus he [obtained] again Syria and Phoenicia.

Unfortunately, the name of the person who accomplished these deeds is broken away from the inscription. Despite other attempts to identify the name of the missing person, no one is so likely a candidate as Quirinius! Thus, if this identification be true, the inscription points to the fact that Quirinius was indeed twice in Syria as a governor. On this interpretation it is likely that Josephus refers to the *second* governorship of Quirinius when he mentions his coming to Syria in A.D. 6.

Did Luke have in mind an earlier governorship of Quirinius, around 8–7 B.C.? If so, it was probably in an extraordinary capacity as a military "trouble shooter" or "legate," since Saturninus was the civil governor at this time.

Coins and the New Testament

Specific coins, called by names which sound strange to us today, are mentioned repeatedly in the New Testament.

The "Widow's Mite."—One of the most inspiring passages in the New Testament concerns the poor widow who gave her last possessions to the Temple treasury: "Jesus sat over against the treasury, and beheld how the people cast money into the treasury: and many that were rich cast in much. And there came a certain poor widow, and she threw in two mites, which make a farthing" (Mark 12:41–42).

The Greek word for "mite," *lepton,* literally means tiny or thin piece. There are several varieties of these "mites" spanning a period of almost two hundred years, from the time of John Hyrcanus (135–105 B.C.) until the period of the first revolt (A.D. 66–70).

During the time of Pilate's governorship, many types of "widow's mites" were current.

Some of Pilate's coins show that he was stubborn in his dealing with the Jews. Other procurators were very accommodating to the Jews in respecting their religious scruples. Therefore, other procurators refused to place offensive symbols on the Jewish coins which were struck under their authority. Not Pilate! He placed objects on his coins that were used in pagan religious ceremonies, perhaps as a deliberate way of irritating his subjects!

Two "Widow's Mites" Issued by Pilate,
Showing Objects Used in Roman Pagan Worship

The "Tribute Penny."—Near the end of Jesus' ministry, his enemies among the Pharisees and the Herodians tried to deceive him by asking him a subtle question:

Is it lawful to give tribute unto Caesar, or not? But Jesus perceived their wickedness, and said, Why tempt ye me, ye hypocrites? Shew me the tribute money. And they brought unto him a penny.

And he saith unto them, Whose is this image and superscription? They say unto him, Caesar's. Then saith he unto them, Render therefore unto Caesar the things which are Caesar's; and unto God the things that are God's (Matt. 22:17-21).

The specific coin shown to Jesus can be determined with great probability. The Greek word for this coin is "denarius," which referred to a silver coin smaller than our quarter. Roman taxes were paid in coins of this value. A denarius represented the amount a man would receive for an average daily wage (see Matt. 20:1-16). The Emperor Augustus minted dozens of varieties of the denarius; Tiberius, on the other hand, issued only three types—two of which are exceedingly rare. The most common denarius of Tiberius was, therefore, most likely the one shown to Jesus in the account of the tribute money (cf. Matt. 22:15-22; Mark 12:13-17; Luke 20:20-26).

The "30 pieces of silver."—Judas received this as payment for betraying Jesus (cf. Matt. 26:14-15). The Roman authorities did not permit Jews in Jesus' day to mint silver coins. Thus, Jews relied on various Phoenician and Egyptian towns for silver coins at this time. Tyre was their most common source. The silver coins of Tyre were of high quality (unlike those of Egypt). A coin of Tyre called a "tetradrachma" or "shekel" was most probably the type which Judas received.

SILVER SHEKEL FROM TYRE

10

The Places of the Gospels

▲▲▲

Geography has rightly been called the "eye of history," for it often supplies the key to a proper understanding of history. Of no other geographical region is this truer than of the biblical countries. Remember how Abraham journeyed all the way from Ur to Haran on his way to Palestine (cf. Gen. 11:31)? This was far out of the way to the north. Palestine appears to be much closer if one would journey west from Ur. But the area which lay between Palestine and Ur is desert, and therefore not suitable for travel. Abraham traveled the established roads, which followed the Euphrates River northwesterly before turning southwest toward Palestine.

The New Testament likewise becomes richer in meaning when its geography is understood. Renan was right when he said that his journey to Palestine was like a "fifth Gospel" to him, since he gained so much through his firsthand observations of the biblical lands. Even though the geography of Palestine has changed somewhat since Renan was there one hundred years ago, his statement is still valid. As a matter of fact, continuing archaeological contributions are making his statement truer today than when he first uttered it.

Herodium

Herodium is a relatively obscure place today; it is located on the edge of the Judean Desert, approximately two and one-half miles south of Bethlehem. At this spot was located one of the numerous palaces of Herod the Great; now it is in ruins. Herodium was built by Herod on his fiftieth birthday (24 B.C.) to serve as a memorial in his honor. Herod, in the early part of his life (40 B.C.), had fought and won a battle here against the Parthians. Because of this great victory, Herodium was a favorite place in Herod's memory, and he even chose to be buried here when he died. Read Matthew's reference to this (2:20).

Herodium has been excavated in three seasons of work (1962–64) by an Italian archaeologist, F. Vergilio Corbo, O.F.M. The most important aspect of this work concerns the information it gives about the luxury and sumptuousness that Herod enjoyed. Jesus made mention of the luxurious clothing that kings wore in their palaces (cf. Matt. 11:8). Now we begin to see other luxuries which members of the Herodian family, in particular, enjoyed.

The excavations have demonstrated that Herod had an elaborate bath system. He could enjoy cold baths, hot baths, warm baths, or sun baths, as desire dictated. Moreover, he had an adjoining dressing room. The walls of his palace were lined with lovely paintings and the floors were richly decorated with artistic mosaics formed by fitting together small chips of colored stone. Herod's mosaics were designed with geometrical patterns, probably to prevent strict Jews from taking offense, which they would if animal designs had been chosen. Jews, of course, were careful to avoid breaking the Second Commandment. It is ironic that Herod has been so largely forgotten, although he took such pains to perpetuate his memory.

Jerusalem

The level of Jerusalem in Jesus' time lies buried beneath many feet of soil and occupational debris of the centuries. It is not possible to excavate Jerusalem on a general scale, since it is still occupied. Many vacant spots within the city, however, have been examined as the opportunities have arisen.

Jerusalem in the time of Jesus must have been very impressive, particularly from the north and from the east. The Mount of Olives overlooked it from the east, and from its top one had a panoramic view of the city. Obviously the road to Bethany ran to the top of the Mount of Olives, past Bethphage, and from thence to Bethany, which was only one and one-half miles distant.

The Praetorium.—There are two main theories concerning the location of this site, where Jesus was brought before Pilate (cf. John 18:28,33; 19:9). One theory equates the Praetorium with the Tower of Antonia, which overlooked the Temple courts on the northwest. During the Jewish festivals, Roman soldiers kept special watch over the grounds of the Temple from the Tower of Antonia, lest any Jewish tumult or revolt break out. Naturally, Roman suspicions were aroused whenever large numbers of the Jewish people assembled together, for bitter experience had shown what could happen. For example, shortly after the death of Herod the Great, the people revolted against his successor, Archelaus, during a Passover gathering at Jerusalem.

The Tower of Antonia is important for its connection with Paul, whether or not it is the actual "Praetorium" where Jesus was tried. Roman soldiers stationed at Antonia took Paul in custody when the Jews caused the tumult over Trophimus (cf. Acts 21:28–36). Paul was kept imprisoned in the "barracks" for a considerable time (cf. Acts 21:34; 23:16).

Yet, the "Praetorium" at Jerusalem, where Pilate stayed when he came from Caesarea to be on hand for the Jewish festivals, was more probably the well-known palace of Herod, on the west side of the city. Here a considerable number of soldiers could be accommodated, in the event of an uprising.

Thus, there were soldiers there who warmed themselves by the fire (see Mark 15:16).

Pilate was an official who had been appointed Procurator of Judea. With the intention of annoying the Jews rather than of honoring Tiberius, he set up gilded shields in Herod's palace in the Holy City. . . . They bore two things . . . the name of the dedicator [Pilate] and that of the person in whose honor the dedication was made [Tiberius] (Philo, *The Embassy to Caligula,* 299).

There is another clue which seems to dictate that the Praetorium refers to Herod's palace. The word "Praetorium" is used to refer to another one of Herod's palaces at Caesarea in Acts 23:35. Paul stayed there while in Caesarea.

Very little archaeological work has been done to recover Herod's palace in Jerusalem. Josephus tells us that the palace had three defense towers on the north—Hippicus, Mariamne, and Phasael. One of these towers still stands, though it is erroneously called the "Tower of David." A British archaeologist named Johns has excavated this tower and has identified it as the ancient tower known as Phasael. One of the most important contributions of his excavations was to demonstrate where the western wall of Jerusalem was located in Jesus' day.

The Pool of Bethesda.—The Pool of Bethesda is mentioned only one time in the Bible: "Now there is at Jerusalem by the sheep market a pool, which is called in the Hebrew tongue Bethesda, having five porches" (John 5:2). Since Josephus said nothing about this pool, some writers were doubtful that the unique reference to Bethesda in John's Gospel could be trusted. Some ancient biblical manuscripts had different readings, such as "Bethsaida," "Belzetha," "Bethzatha," and so on. We know now that John's Gospel was right in reading Bethesda.

In 1870–80, much archaeological work was done at a spot known today as St. Anne's Convent, which was just north of the ancient Temple area. St. Anne's is the first building on the right as a visitor comes into Jerusalem from the eastern gate (St. Stephen's gate). At St. Anne's monastery two large pools were found. Some archaeologists guessed that this was Bethesda, because older writers had said that there were double pools at Bethesda.

For example, Eusebius says (around A.D. 325): "Bethesda, a pool in Jerusalem, which is called the Sheep (Pool), formerly it had five porches. It is now identified with the twin reservoirs, of which one is supplied by the seasonal rains, while the water of the other is a muddy color" (*Onamasticon*, Klostermann, 58, 59).

The Pilgrim of Bordeaux visited Palestine around A.D. 333. He spoke about the "*twin pools*" of Bethesda. One of the most important witnesses to these twin pools was Cyril of Jerusalem, the bishop of Jerusalem. He lived around A.D. 348–86. He wrote: "In Jerusalem there was a Sheep Pool with five porticoes. Four (porticoes) were arranged around about (the pools), the fifth (portico) was arranged through the middle (of the pools); in it lay the sick man" (Migne, *Patr. Gr.*, 33:1133).

More important than any of these later references is one discovered in the Dead Sea Scrolls. It is referred to as having two pools: a smaller basin and a stepped cistern. The scroll which mentions Bethesda dates around A.D. 70. The Copper Document, a scroll written on copper, lists 64 places where there is buried treasure (found in Cave III). One of the places mentioned is Bethesda (italics of the author):

Nearly at *Beth-Eshdatain* [this was the way it was spelled in Hebrew, which means "House of the Two Pools"!], in the reservoir when you enter into the *small basin*: a case of aloes wood (and a vase of) resin from the white pine.

Just nearby, at the western entrance to the lodging of the triclinium (where is found) the platform of the portable stove, close by: nine hundred [talents of silver], five talents of gold sixty talents: on circling around from the west side, beneath the black rock. Nearby, under the threshold of the *stepped cistern,* 42 talents. (Milik's translation, *Discoveries in the Judean Desert* III [Oxford: Clarendon Press, 1962], pp. 297 ff.)

The architectural remains of the pool which have been discovered seem to indicate that Bethesda was constructed about the time of Herod, perhaps with royal patronage.

The Temple of Jerusalem.—Josephus gives confusing information concerning the time Herod began constructing this Temple. In one passage he mentions that it was in Herod's eighteenth year; in another place he says that it was in his fifteenth year. The problem can be solved if in one of the references Josephus reckoned from the time Herod was *officially recognized* as king of Judea (40 B.C.) and in the other reference from the time Herod *actually established* himself as king (37 B.C.) This might mean that construction started around 22 B.C.

Herod's most noteworthy achievement, from the New Testament point of view, was construction of the Temple. This Temple is referred to in the New Testament directly or indirectly over a hundred times. Later Jewish writers also gave much attention to it, and one whole section of the Talmud (called the "Middoth," meaning the "measurements" of the Temple) describes it in great detail. Jewish tradition reported that "he who has not seen Jerusalem in its beauty has not seen a beautiful great city in his whole life; and who has not seen this building of Herod's Temple has not seen a handsome building in his life."

Josephus gives more information than any other source on the construction of Herod's Temple. He mentions that a thousand wagons brought stone; ten thousand skilled workmen were employed; a thousand priests were trained as masons and carpenters to build the sanctuary itself, since common

workmen would ceremonially defile it. The same ground plan
was used for Herod's Temple that was used for Solomon's
(it was 150 feet long); yet, the over-all height of the Temple
was somewhat lower than Solomon's (180 feet) but the front
was twice as high. Work on the sanctuary was finished in
eighteen months. The courts and other constructions, however,
were not finished until A.D. 64. This fact helps New Testament
readers to understand why the Temple construction had been
under way for forty-six years when Jesus carried on his
ministry (see John 2:20).

Several features of Herod's Temple are referred to in the
New Testament; for example, the "Beautiful Gate" (Acts 3:2,
10). Josephus mentions a gate, built out of Corinthian bronze,
on the east side of the Court of Women. This was perhaps
the Beautiful Gate of the New Testament. Corinthian bronze
was an alloy of bronze, silver, and gold. Josephus and the
Talmud mention that a certain Nicanor from Alexandria built
this gate. A first-century Jewish tomb has been found on the
Mount of Olives. One of the bone-chests (ossuaries) seems to
mention him: "[These are] the bones [of the sons] of Nicanor,
who built the gate."

It was at the Beautiful Gate that Peter and John healed the
crippled man (cf. Acts 3:2). There is some evidence to indicate that at this time cripples were not only excluded from
the temple courts of Israel but also from synagogue worship,
since their suffering was interpreted as punishment from God
(see 2 Sam. 5:8). Women were forbidden to sit with the
men in the synagogues and were screened off out of sight.
This is likely why this cripple was forced to sit at the gate to
the Court of Women.

Matthew's reference to the "pinnacle of the Temple" (4:5)
has been interpreted in various ways. Most writers relate this
reference to the southeast angle of the Temple courts, which
stood above the Kidron Valley at a height of over three

hundred feet. Josephus says that anyone who looked down from this spot would become dizzy. Others have interpreted the pinnacle as the top of the sanctuary itself; still others as the top of one of the gateways of the Temple.

The "Synagogue of the Libertines."—In Acts 6:9, mention is made of Stephen's disputes with certain members of a synagogue of the "Libertines." The word "Libertine" which is used here means freedmen; that is, it refers to Jews who had been in slavery but had been freed.

In December, 1913, R. Weill excavated in the southeastern part of Jerusalem and found an inscription that seems to refer to a synagogue of the "freedmen." It reads:

Theodotus [Hebrew "Jonathan" or "Nathaniel"] [son] of Vettenius, a priest and ruler of the synagogue, son of a ruler of the synagogue, grandson of a ruler of the synagogue, has built the synagogue for the reading of [the] law and for [the] teaching of the commandments and the guest chambers and the constructions and the water installation for a lodging place to those visitors from abroad who have need. His paternal ancestors and the elders and Simonides have laid the foundations.

Theodotus was the son or grandson of a Jew who had taken a Latin name. Probably it comes from a well-known Latin family—Vettia or Vettena. In the time of Pompey great numbers of Jewish citizens had been taken into slavery. Likely Vettenius had been taken about that time. When he gained his freedom and returned to his homeplace, he still retained the name of the family he had served.

This inscription probably dates to around A.D. 50 or before. It refers to certain rooms and conveniences provided for Jewish pilgrims who would come to Jerusalem for the festivals. It was a common custom at this time for synagogues to have such accommodations, as the inscription itself indicates. The same word used on the inscription (*kataluma*—meaning lodging place) was used by Luke to refer to the "inn" which had "no room" for Mary and Joseph (cf. Luke 2:7). Was Mary refused room in a synagogue hostel?

Nazareth

The name "Nazareth" means watch place and probably was so called because of its elevation (1100 feet) in relation to the Valley of Esdraelon, which was located only two miles to the south.

Nazareth is famous as the place where Jesus grew to manhood (cf. Luke 2:39–40). Here history could jump out at him in panoramic fashion. To the west he could see all the way to Carmel, where Elijah refuted the prophets of Baal; to the south he could glimpse the sinister mound of Megiddo, which was not occupied in his time but was the scene of many battles—such as the one fought in 608 B.C. between Josiah, the Judean King, and Necho, the Egyptian King; to the southeast he could observe Gilboa (where Jonathan and Saul were killed) and Tabor, where Deborah and Barak assembled their troops to fight Sisera.

Parts of Nazareth are still located on the northern hillside. But the main part is centered in a bowl-shaped valley.

In recent years many radical critics have questioned the New Testament statements that Jesus grew up in Nazareth. Since neither the Old Testament, Josephus, nor the Talmud refers to Nazareth, these writers point out, it must not have been in existence in the New Testament period. This argument can stand no longer.

The Italian archaeologist Bagatti has done extensive excavating there and has discovered that Nazareth was indeed a town in the time of Jesus, and long before as well. On the basis of pottery discovered, he was able to trace the town's settlement back to a time before 1200 B.C.

The author was privileged to be in charge of some excavations in Caesarea in 1962. Various important discoveries were made, but by far the most important was the discovery of an inscription which mentioned Nazareth. It was written in Hebrew and dated to a time around A.D. 250–300. The inscription was discovered almost by accident, since it was recovered from a wheelbarrow with debris about to be discarded!

The main substance of the inscription dealt with various Galilean villages where the priestly families (see 1 Chron. 24:15) settled after Jerusalem's destruction in A.D. 70. Since these migrations of the priests to Galilee took place in the first and second centuries, the inscription is a valuable historical document, for it shows that Nazareth was settled in the early Roman period. Various first-century Jewish tombs have also been discovered at Nazareth. Thus, the evidence for its habitation in Jesus' time is more respectable than ever before.

Chorazin

Chorazin is spoken of as one of the places which had been particularly blessed, since Jesus did so many miracles there (cf. Matt. 11:21; Luke 10:13). Its exact location is disputed. In 1857, a British explorer named Thompsen identified this city with a ruined site called Kerazeh, which is located about two miles due north of the Sea of Galilee. This theory has been generally accepted but there is a problem connected with it.

In recent years, an Israeli archaeologist, Zeev Yeivin, has carried out extensive excavations at Kerazeh.

The town was planned in such a way that it had two main intersecting roads—one running north and south and the other east and west. A synagogue was located directly at the meeting point of these two roads. Yeivin's excavations have been concentrated around this synagogue, which was built of black, volcanic rock (basalt) with superb artistic decorations.

The most important discovery found at the synagogue at Kerazeh is that of a "seat of Moses." During their instructions in the synagogue services, the teachers of the period sat in a chair before the congregation (see Matt. 23:2). The funds to make this chair and other synagogue areas had been donated by a prominent member, according to the inscription written on it: "Blessed be the memory of Judah son of Ishmael who made the porch and staircase and completed the work. May there come to him a share with the righteous."

Thus, whether Kerazeh can be established as the true Chorazin of the New Testament or not, the value of this "seat of Moses" is outstanding for its relationship to the reference in Matthew.

Perhaps there were two "Chorazins," since towns sometimes moved from one place to another. Kerazeh itself could well be the site mentioned in the Talmud as the place where the wheat ripened early.

Cana in Galilee

Cana in Galilee is one of the places mentioned in the Gospels which has never been excavated. But intensive surface examinations have been made in recent years at a spot called Khirbet Qana. On the basis of the pottery found, this abandoned site seven miles north of Nazareth is to be equated with Cana in Galilee (mentioned in John 2:1; 4:46; 21:2). The periods of occupation represented by the pottery fit those periods in which Cana was occupied.

We know from literary references that as early as Tiglath Pileser, an Assyrian king who reigned between 745-27 B.C., Cana was well occupied. Tiglath Pileser says he captured a "Cana" in Galilee around 732 B.C. and took 650 prisoners. The period between 900 and 600 B.C. is known to archaeologists as "Iron II." Much pottery is found at Cana from this period. The New Testament references and Josephus (who lived there for a while) demonstrate that Cana was likewise occupied in the early Roman period (63 B.C.–A.D. 150). Again the pottery is abundant for this time and all the other periods when literary sources indicate Cana was settled.

Another site, Kefer Kenna, located five miles east of Nazareth, has been identified by many authorities as Cana. However, there is neither sufficient archaeological nor literary evidence to support this.

11

The Journeys of Paul

▲▲▲

Around A.D. 1800, only one of the cities visited by Paul on his first missionary journey in Asia Minor could be identified with certainty. The recovery of these cities, as well as other places which relate to Paul's life, has been due to the labors of many. Inscriptions have been of special importance in locating several of these places mentioned in the book of Acts and in Paul's epistles.

Tarsus

Tarsus was the city where Paul was born (cf. Acts 22:3). Paul was indeed right when he said that it was "no average city" (cf. Acts 21:39). Tarsus was located near the Cilician Gates, a series of mountain passes across the Taurus Mountains, which began about thirty miles north of Tarsus. Thus, it was a strategic city. Also, it commanded the roads which converged upon it from all directions.

Hetty Goldman, an American archaeologist, over many seasons of excavations has discovered that a site stood at Tarsus long before the time of Homer. Her work mostly dealt with the pre-Christian period; but, it is interesting to realize that Tarsus was already referred to in the records of ancient Assyrian and Babylonian kings as an important city during the time of the ninth to the sixth centuries B.C.

Strabo, the famous geographer, has given us much valuable information about Tarsus in the time of Paul. He mentions the high intelligence of the schools of philosophy there and tells us that Athenodorus, the teacher of the Roman Emperor Augustus, came from Tarsus.

On the Taurus range of mountains a particular kind of longhaired goat was raised. A fine material called "cilicium" was produced from the hair of these goats and was used especially for sailcloth and tent cloth. Paul probably learned the tentmaking craft from his background at Tarsus. Other scholars argue that Paul was a leather worker.

Antioch in Syria

Antioch in Syria was one of the earliest cities outside Judea where the gospel was first proclaimed. There the disciples of Jesus were "first called Christians" (Acts 11:26). In the first century, Antioch had a large number of wealthy Jews who gave liberally for the support of the Temple at Jerusalem. Therefore, Antioch had strong connections with Judea.

Antioch was located on the Orontes River, about twenty miles inland from the coast. The port of Antioch, Seleucia, was located at the mouth of the Orontes. It will be remembered that Paul sailed out from Seleucia when he set out on his first missionary journey (see Acts 13:4).

Much of Antioch is still occupied, which prevents excavations. However, the city is much smaller (only 45,000 population) than it was in the time of Paul, when it was the third city of the Roman Empire—only Rome and Alexandria were larger.

In 1932, excavations were carried on at Antioch under the patronage of Princeton University, the Worcester Art Museum, and the National Museum of France. Most of the discoveries of this team related to a period after the first century. However, a few of the finds, particularly some beautiful mosaic floors, reached back to the New Testament era. Most often pictured were the aspirations and superstitious religious beliefs of the time. The pagan gods—such as Hermes, Baccus, Heracles—are usually shown in connection with some of their famous deeds. For example, Baccus is engaged in a drinking contest in one of these mosaics. Thus these mosaics are important for the light they give about the luxury, as well as the religious concepts, which prevailed at Antioch in Paul's day.

Derbe

The exact location of Derbe has been determined only recently. Older attempts to identify the place were completely futile. In 1957, archaeological explorer M. Ballance found an inscription which settled the matter. Dated around A.D. 156–57, the inscription was dedicated to the Emperor Antoninus Pius by the people of "Claudio-Derbe." The present name of the mound where Derbe has been located correctly is Kerti Hüyük.

The most significant thing about this new identification is that Derbe was much nearer Tarsus than formerly realized (it is 35 miles closer than all maps show it). This fact helps us to see Paul in a new perspective. It would have been very easy and much safer for Paul, when he reached the limit of his first missionary journey, to journey straight on to Tarsus. Derbe lay directly on the main road there and it was only a few days' journey away. Paul had just passed through serious dangers (he was nearly killed by stoning at Lystra). Moreover, there was a good road all the way to Antioch in Syria via Tarsus; and, it was much shorter. But, when he arrived in Derbe, Paul decided to return the way he had come. This he did to strengthen his young converts in their new-found Christian faith (cf. Acts 14:20–23).

Lystra

The location of Lystra, like so many of the places Paul visited on his first missionary journey, was unknown for centuries. In 1820, William M. Leake, an outstanding British authority on ancient geography, conjectured accurately that Lystra was located near a place known today as Khatyn Serai. In 1884, an American archaeologist, J. R. S. Sterrett, found a Latin inscription which definitely proved that Leake was correct. The inscription reads: "The Colony, Julia Felix Gemina Lystra, has consecrated the sacred Augusteum by the decree of the decuriones."

The coins of Lystra, inscribed in Latin, also speak of it as the "Colony, Julia Felix Gemina Lystra." Some of Lystra's early coins also seem to show that Latin was not too familiar to the people there. Some letters on Lystra's coins are made backward and some words are misspelled. This throws some light on Luke's statement that the common people of Lystra spoke Lycaonian (cf. Acts 14:11).

It is easy to understand why the people of Lystra would identify Paul with Hermes and Barnabas with Jupiter and treat them so well (cf. Acts 14:12). These gods had supposedly appeared in this region at one time, but most of the citizens refused to be kind to them, since these gods were not recognized by the people. An old couple named Philemon and Baucis treated these gods hospitably, sharing their food with them. Jupiter and Hermes, according to the legend, later sent a flood to destroy all the unworthy people but spared Philemon and Baucis.

Antioch in Pisidia

Paul journeyed to Antioch in Pisidia from Perga, on the southern shore of Asia Minor. The road between these two places was dangerous, since many bandits infested the roads.

Paul could well have had this section of road in mind when he wrote that he was sometimes "in perils of robbers" (2 Cor. 11:26).

Antioch in Pisidia was first identified, in 1833, by Francis J. Arundell, a British chaplain stationed in Smyrna. Today it is called Yalovatch. Following a clue of William M. Leake, who had correctly located Lystra, Arundell found certain inscriptions at Yalovatch which established that it was Antioch in Pisidia. Antioch was located in a fertile plain on the banks of the Anthius River, with a magnificent view of mountains (called the Sultan Dagh today) to the north. Remains of an aqueduct which brought water down from these mountains still stand.

David M. Robinson, an American archaeologist, had notable success excavating at Antioch. He found important inscriptions which filled out the historical account of the Emperor Augustus.

Robinson also found two large courtyards in the center of the city. One was dedicated to Augustus; the other, to Tiberius. One of his most interesting finds was an inscription which dated from Domitian's time. This inscription forbade speculation in grain, since it was scarce due to a hard winter (see Rev. 6:6–8). The many Latin inscriptions which were found show how strongly Latin influence had already penetrated this city, which excavations have shown to be a town of great wealth.

Philippi

On his second missionary journey, the first two cities Paul visited were Neapolis and Philippi. Neapolis was the port and Philippi was located inland around sixteen miles. The original name of Philippi was Krenides. In the beginning it was very small but after it came into the possession of Philip, father of Alexander the Great, in 360 B.C., it was enlarged and renamed. It became important because of nearby gold mines.

In the New Testament period Philippi became famous as the place where, in 42 B.C., Anthony and Octavian (later Augustus) defeated Brutus and Cassius, the murderers of Julius Caesar. Philippi was greatly enlarged, since it was made into a colony: "Philippi, which is the leading city of the district of Macedonia, and a Roman colony" (Acts 16:12, RSV). The coins of Philippi likewise mention it as a colony and an inscription also has been discovered which refers to it as the "Colony of Julia Augusta Philippi."

Excavations were carried on at Philippi by the French School of Athens in 1914–38. Greek archaeologists are continuing to find various inscriptions which indicate that a great number of people from different regions lived there—Romans, Egyptians, Thracians, Greeks, and so on. Many gods were worshiped, such as Isis, Cybele, Athena, and others. It occasions no surprise, therefore, to read of Lydia, a seller of purple, from Thyatira, as dwelling in Philippi (cf. Acts 16:14). A Latin inscription has been found which mentions "purple dyers." This shows that a guild of these merchants lived there.

It was customary for Jews to build a "house of prayer" (or, even a synagogue) on a river or a seashore. The synagogue at Caesarea, which the author helped to excavate in 1962, was located directly on the shore of the Mediterranean. The riverside mentioned in Acts 16:13 refers to the Gangites River, which flowed past Philippi about a mile to the west. It would be permissible for Jews to worship there, since it lay outside the city boundary where Roman law required houses of strange cults to be located.

Thessalonica

Much archaeological work has been done in Thessalonica, but it deals mostly with a period later than the New Testament era. One of the most interesting discoveries here is that of an inscription which refers to the "rulers of the city" by the same word which Luke uses—"politarchs". This inscription is today in the British Museum. Other Macedonian inscriptions have been found which refer to "politarchs," which was the regular term employed in Macedonian cities by which to designate their city officials.

Athens

In 27 B.C. Corinth replaced Athens as capital of Greece. So, at the time of Paul's visit (A.D. 49–50), Athens was a philosophical, university town, "resting on its past laurels." It was described by Luke as a city given to idolatry (cf. Acts 17:1). Nero, who became Roman Emperor in A.D. 52, was aware of the rich Athenian art treasures. He had many of them carried off to Rome during the course of his reign.

Thus far, no inscription has been found which refers to the "unknown God" (Acts 17:23). However, in the excavations at Pergamum, an inscription was found which reads: "To *Gods* unknown, [by] Capito, a torch bearer." Other ancient writers refer to dedications of a similar type.

One of the most interesting questions of Paul's visit to Athens concerns the identification of "Mars hill" (Acts 17:22). This reference could refer either to a council of dignitaries or to a special hill where this council met in an older time. An inscription found in 1952 speaks of the "Areopagus" as meeting in a council chamber near the market place. This inscription dates from 337–336 B.C. Paul, of course, was in the market place when he met the Stoics and Epicureans (cf. Acts 17:18). It is possible, however, that Paul and these philosophers walked to a hill a short distance away (only a few hundred yards) to hear Paul deliver his famous sermon. Thus, Paul could well have gestured toward the Acropolis,

an adjoining hill which was crowned with beautiful temples—
Parthenon, Theseum, and so on—when he made his point
that God "dwelleth not in temples made with hands" (17:24).

Corinth

Corinth was one of the most famous cities which Paul
visited. It was destroyed in 146 B.C. by a Roman general
named Mummius. After this it lay in ruins for over a century.
In 44 B.C. Julius Caesar authorized its rebuilding. Its official
name became *Laus Iulia Corinthus,* in his honor. In 27 B.C.
Corinth became the capital of Greece; it remained so throughout the New Testament period. This new city of Corinth
was strongly touched with Roman influence and a large part
of the first-century inscriptions found there are in Latin.
Likewise, all of Corinth's coins in the New Testament period
bear Latin legends.

Corinth owed its greatness to its strategic location. It lay
near a narrow neck of land, the Isthmus of Corinth, which
connected southern Greece with the northern mainland. Thus,
both sea traffic and land traffic were brought to Corinth.
Moreover, considerable time was saved by mariners who
preferred to pass over the Isthmus of Corinth rather than to
sail around southern Greece (which was dangerous). Their
boats were lifted out of the water onto a dolly, which was
pulled over a curbed, flagstone road called the "Diolkos."
A Greek archaeologist who recently excavated this roadway
has demonstrated that it was first built before 600 B.C.

Corinth had a notorious reputation for immorality. Aphrodite, the goddess of love was worshiped here. The historian
Strabo mentions that a thousand priestesses served this goddess by using their bodies for immoral purposes. The temple
of Aphrodite stood on top of the mountain called "Acrocorin-
thus," which overlooked Corinth.

Since 1898, Corinth has witnessed excavations which have
been conducted by the American School of Classical Studies

in Athens. The archaeological discoveries at Corinth have been of great interest for their bearing on the New Testament. One Latin inscription mentions the "meat market" of which Paul spoke (called the "shambles" in 1 Cor. 10:25).

Acts 18:12 speaks about the "judgment seat" or "tribunal" of Gallio. This "judgment seat," called the "rostrum" on an inscription, has likewise been excavated and can be seen today. Gallio held court in a large public square on the south side of the market place (Agora). This platform on which Gallio and other Roman governors sat was very impressive and ornamental.

Since legal cases were tried in a large open space, friends of the persons who were on trial would often assemble in great numbers and try to influence the decision of the Roman governor by audibly protesting or agreeing with him. A similar type trial was carried on in the case of Jesus before Pilate. Gallio, unlike Pilate, was firm and refused to give in to popular sentiment (cf. Acts 18:14–17).

An inscription has also been discovered which possibly refers to the same "Erastus" who is mentioned in Romans 16:23. Paul's letter to the Romans was written from Corinth, and this fact gives a vivid background to the kind of depravity described in Romans 1. Also, mention should be made of an inscription (dating around A.D. 150), which refers to the "Synagogue of the Hebrews." The lettering of the inscription is roughly made and seems to indicate that the Jewish group at Corinth was rather poor and of low estate. Paul says the Christians of Corinth were likewise mostly poor (cf. 1 Cor. 1:26–31) and many of these Christians came out of the Jewish synagogue at Corinth.

Ephesus

Ephesus was one of the four greatest cities in the world in the time of Paul (the others were Rome, Alexandria, and Antioch). It was famous as the place where the temple of

Diana (or "Artemis") was located, and this temple was one of the "seven wonders" of the ancient world. Archaeological discoveries at Ephesus which relate to the New Testament have been of great importance.

J. T. Wood, an English architect, went to Ephesus in 1863 to look for the lost temple of Artemis. He gained a clue to its location by finding an inscription in the theater at Ephesus which told that on May 25, the birthday of Artemis, silver images of her would be brought in by one entrance to the theater (the Magnesian Gate) and taken out by another exit (the Coressian Gate). He followed the road by which the images were taken away and in 1869 finally found the lost site of the famous temple. More work on this temple of Artemis was also carried out by David Hogarth in 1904.

In more recent years Austrian archaeologists likewise have done much work on the theater at Ephesus. This theater is referred to in Acts 19:29 as the place where Demetrius and his fellow silversmiths raised such a disturbance against Paul. The inscriptions found by Wood seem to clarify the meaning of the New Testament reference to these silver images. Also, in recent years, certain impressive marble statues of Diana have been found in Ephesus. As Wood's inscription demonstrates, it seems that these silversmiths grew rich, since wealthy patrons would often provide enormous sums and endowments to have these statues made and cared for so that they could be paraded in the annual birthday celebrations of Artemis.

The theater had vast dimensions. It was about 450 by 325 feet. It could hold approximately twenty-five thousand people, which exceeds the eighteen thousand-capacity of Madison Square Garden. The book of Acts (19:32,39,41) designates the multitude which had assembled in the theater as an *ecclēsia*, which is the same word that is elsewhere in the New Testament translated "church." However, the inscriptions found in this theater also designate those who assembled there as the *ecclēsia*, which explains why Luke used this term here as he did. Of course, "assembly" is the basic meaning behind the Greek word which is translated "church" in the New Testament.

Caesarea

At the end of Paul's third missionary journey, he landed at Caesarea on his way to Jerusalem (cf. Acts 21:8). Caesarea is located on the Mediterranean coast approximately seventy miles northwest of Jerusalem. It was founded around 25-22 B.C. on the old, destroyed site of a Phoenician colony named Strato's Tower. Herod the Great, who built this port, named it "Caesarea" in honor of Augustus Caesar. It was to serve as Herod's main connecting link with Rome. Caesarea is referred to fifteen times in the book of Acts. It was the Roman capital of Judea and Samaria in Jesus' day; thus Pilate had his main residence there.

Numerous archaeological campaigns have been conducted at Caesarea. It is an ideal place for excavations since it is today largely abandoned. Although little of the total area available has been excavated, some outstanding discoveries have been made.

The defense wall of Caesarea is especially important. It was seen by Peter and Paul in their many visits to Caesarea. Perhaps Cornelius the centurion, the first Gentile to become a Christian (see Acts 10), helped to maintain the defenses of this wall. At short intervals circular defense towers projected high above the wall and out from it. These towers thus gave a great advantage to the defenders of Caesarea in the event of an attack. The stones used in constructing the wall were well-squared. These were quarried at the southern end of the Carmel Mountain range (Kabbara), which begins only three miles north of Caesarea.

The theater where King Agrippa (see Acts 12:25) was smitten with his fatal illness has likewise been recovered. The very place where Agrippa was supposedly standing when he made his speech was the governor's "box-seat"; this spot can now be seen by visitors to this theater. On the orchestra floor of the theater, various painted murals have been discovered. Many of the original theater seats which were fashioned by Herod's workmen have likewise been recovered. The inscription mentioning Pilate (referred to earlier) was found in this theater.

Just outside the theater a marble statue of Diana or Artemis of Ephesus was discovered. Acts 19:27 mentions that the great goddess was worshiped all over the world. Coins from thirty different Greco-Roman cities indeed demonstrate that Artemis was widely acclaimed, and this statue of her which was recovered in a faraway Palestinian city adds extra weight to the older evidence of her popularity.

Caesarea's harbor, into which Paul sailed and from which he went to Rome (cf. Acts 27:2), is vividly pictured on a coin which was found by an underwater team of archaeologists, led by Edwin Link in 1960.

On the Way to Rome

It is not convenient here to describe in detail all the spots visited by Paul nor the vivid account of his shipwreck as given in Acts 27 and 28. However, some mention of Paul's route after landing in Italy is in order.

Puteoli (cf. Acts 28:13) was one of Rome's major ports. It had been renamed in honor of Nero, but the older name was still in vogue and was resumed again after Nero's disgraceful death. Located about 170 miles south of Rome, today Puteoli is called Pozzuoli, being part of the modern suburbs north of Naples. An ancient glass bottle has been discovered which shows roughly how Puteoli looked in Paul's day. It is also pictured on a wall mural from Pompeii, which

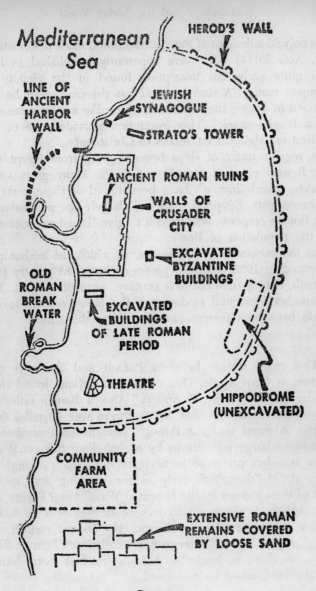

Mediterranean Sea

HEROD'S WALL

LINE OF ANCIENT HARBOR WALL

JEWISH SYNAGOGUE

STRATO'S TOWER

ANCIENT ROMAN RUINS

WALLS OF CRUSADER CITY

EXCAVATED BYZANTINE BUILDINGS

OLD ROMAN BREAK WATER

EXCAVATED BUILDINGS OF LATE ROMAN PERIOD

THEATRE

HIPPODROME (UNEXCAVATED)

COMMUNITY FARM AREA

EXTENSIVE ROMAN REMAINS COVERED BY LOOSE SAND

CAESAREA

was only 25 miles east of Puteoli. Mention is made of Christians (cf. Acts 28:14) who were apparently established in Puteoli quite early. An inscription found in the vicinity of Pompeii reads: "A strange mind has driven A. and he has pressed in among the Christians who make a man a prisoner as a laughingstock." This inscription provides one of the earliest extrabiblical references to Christianity.

A regular traffic of ships brought grain from Egypt into the Roman cities of Puteoli and Ostia. Many grain warehouses, called "horrea", have been found at these ports by archaeologists. Egyptian grain was largely the possession of the Roman emperor, who used it to give "bread and circuses" to the population of Rome.

In the excavations of Caesarea, in which the author participated in 1962, beautiful pieces of inscribed pottery from Puteoli, dating from the first century, were discovered. This is another incidental evidence of the heavy sea traffic and trade between Caesarea and Puteoli at this time.

Appii Forum

This small station between Puteoli and Rome is now known as Foro Appio. One of the inscriptions found there reads: "At the Forum of Appius." Also, a Roman milestone found there indicates that Appii Forum was 43 miles from Rome. A canal was cut through swamps and marshes. A passenger barge was drawn by mules along this canal and most travelers preferred to navigate this region at night so they could "disembark early in the morning and go the rest of their journey by the [Appian] Way." Appii Forum, like the Appian Way on which it was located, was named in honor of Appius Claudius Caecus, the famous censor, who lived around 312 b.c. The swamps, called the Pontine Marshes, are there no longer since Mussolini had them drained so the land could be reclaimed.

Horace (*Satires* I.V.III.6) described the discomforts of travel in the vicinity of Appii Forum. Hotel lodging was expensive, frogs made terrible noises, and the mosquitoes were unendurable! It is easy to understand why Paul would be glad to welcome Christian brethren at Three Taverns (cf. Acts 28:15) after his miserable trip through the marshes. Three Taverns was about ten miles north of Appii Forum. It was also located on the Appian Road, an excellent highway between Rome and Brindisi, in the southern "heel" of Italy.

Rome

In the time of Paul, Rome had over four million residents, a large portion of whom were slaves. It was a grand city spread out, according to Pliny (*Natural History* III, 66–67), over an area which would require sixty miles to encompass in a straight line or about twenty miles in diameter. Before the Emperor Augustus came to power, Rome was sadly lacking in architectural grandeur. The Roman historian Suetonius reports that Augustus so improved Rome's appearance that he boasted: "I found Rome built of sun-dried bricks; I leave her clothed in marble."

H. J. Leon, a leading authority on the subject, has calculated that fifty thousand Jews were in Rome when Paul visited there. Luke informs us that Paul quickly established contact with the Jewish leaders at Rome (see Acts 28:17).

Many inscriptions have been found in the Jewish catacombs. These inscriptions attest to the Jews' belief during the Roman period in a life after death. Unlike their pagan neighbors, Jews never cremated (Christians followed the Jews in their burial practices). The bones of the deceased were saved and stored in underground catacomb crypts to await the day of resurrection. A funeral text from a Jewish crypt is dedicated by a loving husband to his departed wife:

Here is buried Regina. . . . She is sure to live again, and again return to the light [of life]; for she can have hope of this, because she shall rise for a promised eternity, which is the unfailing faith of the worthy and pious. She deserved to have an abode in the blessed country. This will be assured you by your chaste life, your love for your people, your faithfulness to the Law, the purity of your wedded life. . . .

(This Jewish concept of attaining eternal life by one's righteousness, however, has no place in Paul's thought. See Romans 3:20.)

It was not always easy to maintain one's virtue in Rome, as this Jewish wife had done. Even in high society, the most degrading practices were followed. The pages of Roman writers such as Ovid, Petronius, Juvenal, and Martial supply shocking information about the prevalence of prostitution in Rome at this time. Paul was also aware of the notorious depravity of Rome, as seen in the first chapter of his letter to the Romans. Morality in general was trampled in the dust.

Juvenal (VI. 638) states that Messalina, the wife of the Emperor Claudius, used to slip away from the imperial palace at night (under an assumed name of Lycisca) and practice immorality at a harlot's cell. Julia, the only daughter of Augustus, lived such a scandalous life that Augustus banished her (Suetonius, *Augustus* 65) to the miserable island of Ventotene. According to Suetonius, Augustus' life was just as bad (*Augustus* 68–71).

The stories related by Suetonius about Nero, the Roman Emperor before whom Paul was tried, are incredible. He even had his own mother Agrippina killed (*Nero*, 34) and his stepbrother Brittanicus poisoned. He was guilty of homosexuality, rape, murder, bribery, and sadism. It is easy to understand why Rome would be called the "mother of harlots" (cf. Rev. 17:5). Much immorality was even practiced in the name of religion.

It is difficult to know where Paul stayed in Rome. In Philippians 1:13, he seems to imply that he stayed in another "Praetorium." This is possibly a reference to the Praetorian Camp, which was in the northeastern area of Rome.

The Jews of Rome had numerous synagogues. Numerous inscriptions have come to light which mention some of these synagogues. We read of synagogues of the Augusteans, the Volumnians, the Agrippensians, the Herodians, the Campesians, the Syburesians, the Vernaculi, the Calcaremians, the Tripolitans, the Elaians, the Sekeni, and so on. One inscription mentions the Synagogue of the Hebrew: "Here lies Salome daughter of Gaddea, father of the Synagogue of the Hebrews. She lived forty-one years. In peace be her sleep."

Archaeological work has just been carried out on a newly-discovered Jewish synagogue at Ostia. Ostia, like Puteoli, was another seaport which served Rome. It was located at the mouth of the Tiber (the word "Ostia" means mouth), about fourteen miles to the southwest of Rome.

The synagogue at Ostia was discovered accidentally while engineers were building a road. This is the earliest synagogue ever discovered in Europe, for its foundations date to around A.D. 50. Only one other synagogue has been discovered that can claim to be as old as this. In his 1963 excavations at Masada, on the southern end of the Dead Sea, Y. Yadin found a Jewish synagogue which dates sometime before A.D. 70.

For Further Reading

▲▲▲

Additional information, maps, or pictures can be found in the following books:

Albright, *Archaeology and the Religion of Israel* (Johns Hopkins), on Old Testament.

Albright, *The Archaeology of Palestine* (Penguin), comprehensive treatment of discoveries, paperback.

Bouquet, *Everyday Life in New Testament Times* (Scribner).

Finegan, *Light from the Ancient Past* (Princeton), on Old and New Testaments.

The Good News (American Bible Society), edition of New Testament with helpful illustrations.

Kenyon, *Archaeology in the Holy Land* (Praeger), on Old Testament, paperback available.

Kramer, *History Begins at Sumer* (Doubleday-Anchor), background of Old Testament, paperback.

Pritchard, *The Ancient Near East: An Anthology of Texts and Pictures* (Princeton), background of Old Testament.

Thompson, *Archaeology and the New Testament* (Eerdmans).

Wright, *Biblical Archaeology* (Westminster), Old and New Testaments, abridged paperback available.

Wright and Filson, *The Westminster Historical Atlas to the Bible* (Westminster).